"Never Trust a God Over 30"
New Styles in Campus Ministry

"Never Trust a God Over 30"

New Styles in Campus Ministry

Edited by

Albert H. Friedlander

Introduction by Paul Goodman

McGraw-Hill Book Company

NEW YORK   TORONTO   LONDON   SYDNEY

Library of Congress catalog card number 67-24436
FIRST EDITION
22430

CONTENTS

CONTENTS

Introduction: Chaplains and Students
PAUL GOODMAN

When I was in college, class of '31, we thought—justifiably or not—that a student going in for the ministry was probably a moron, intellectually on the level of candidate for officer in the Army, but less sexy. Today, the estimate would be that he is more intellectual and probably more spirited than the average. I can think of several reasons for the change.

At present, a thoughtful and spirited young person who wants to be a professional might gravitate to the ministry *faute de mieux*, since most of the other professions have become arid or morally unacceptable. Medicine still has a noble image, though tarnished. Education, clinical psychology, and architecture are attractive, but the conditions for practicing them are increasingly dubious. Law looks pretty venal. The physical sciences have become too specialized and are grimly and increasingly tied to war. Engineering has lost its glamour since there is so much technology that is misused. Diplomated social work and much sociology seem more like rackets than professions. Scholarship—being a college professor—seems to be just hanging on in school and not having a vocation at all. There are statistics that show a drift of bright and imaginative collegians from field to field: they start with engineering because they have a knack for it and it promises good money; they transfer to pure science but find it humanly unsatisfactory; they fall into the social sciences and are disillusioned; they end up in the humanities—and often then drop out. The ministry is partly being in the humanities and partly dropping out.

The possibility of tailor-making the conditions of practice is one attraction of the ministry. In other professions there has been a steady tendency for professionals to become professional personnel, agents of a bureaucracy or organization that determines policy and defines practice—as on the Highway Commission or The New York Board of Education, or with Merck or Skidmore, Owings and Merrill—so that responsibility and ethical relation to client and community get lost in the shuffle. In the ministry the present historical tendency is in the other direction. Organization is loosening—even among the Roman Catholics—and a minister has a chance of shaping his ministry according to his lights. Thus, if a young man feels himself directed to progressive education, psychology, community development, theater, legal aid, politics, he can reasonably hope to practice more freely in the ministry than in the school system, the Welfare Department, the Democratic party, or on Broadway. At least there are shining examples of such freer and better practice. Church real estate, endowments, scholarships, and grants are often peculiarly free-floating at present. For instance, there are interesting cases where a church group serves as a broker with the poverty program and then transmits the money for real democracy or education, which would be impossible without church sponsorship. Just because society has become more "secular," the physical church is less limited by the secular Establishment: its social functions have become fuzzy, but its nostalgic ideal, its tax exemption, and its real estate persist; so it is again open to enterprise and spirit.

With dismaying rapidity during the past thirty years, society has become dehumanized. One can tick off the horrors: the Spanish War, World War II, the gas chambers, the atom bomb, the Cold War, the stockpiling of atom bombs, the Frankenstein-monster technology, the unecological urbanization, the cumbersome centralization, the social engineering, the mass communications, the processing education, the trivializing of democracy. It is in this context that the professions have lost their humane spirit. By contrast the church, so long a pillar of orthodox society, has begun to recall, dimly, that it has something to do with humanity, with persons, with divinity. And young people of intellect and spirit, who cannot breathe in the ambience of dehumanization and factory-education, are often willing to hang around the chaplain. Again *faute de mieux*. He may be a chump but he is not a machine, and he *might* be serious. For instance, if one wants to talk for real, in terms of happiness and duty, about sexual morals or the drug laws, it is useless to go to the school psychologist or a member of the American Medical Association, but one might have a meeting at the existentialist chaplain's. I never expected to see the day when the church would be the leader in "immorality!"

For someone going into the ministry on the basis of these considerations, a campus post makes a lot of sense. It is certainly not an escape from the world, as some touchingly fear, if only because half our population is under twenty-six, forty per cent of the college-age group is in college, six million at present; and these students, the dominant inheritors of our society, are the best hope, finally the sole hope, of altering our doom-bound career. Of course a campus post *is* a trap if the young chaplain has never really left school, if he has just continued in the academic environment like any other instructor and assistant professor. The campus is something to return to when one has made connections and taken on duties outside the campus.

Universities must be regarded both as schools for apprentice professionals and as communities of the young. In both respects a campus minister has a major task. Given the narrow specialization, know-how orientation, and preparation of organization men that characterize most professional training, there is a need to seek the human meaning of the professions. This ought to be the function of "the community of scholars" itself, but on most campuses there is no such community. There is no dialogue of the professors across their disciplines; the disciplines are not philosophically conceived; and the students are working for union cards. Take questions like the following: What happens to medicine in present urban conditions? What is the ethical and community responsibility of civil engineers? What is the responsibility of lawyers to change the laws under which they practice, so that justice may be done? What should the division of humanities be doing about television? Does it make a difference to physics that the bulk of money for research and development is military? It is an amazing and melancholy fact of American universities that such essentially *professional* questions are likely to be discussed, if at all, in the YMCA or Hillel, not in the departments or divisions. If a minister means to serve where the need is, this is where the need is.

The majority of students, needless to say, are not in college for academic or professional reasons at all. The fact remains that there are these hundreds of communities of many thousands of young people, a social phenomenon unique in history. What can these communities make of themselves? They have potentially a solidarity of peer loyalty and common interests in a society from which the young feel pretty alienated. Also, although the academic processing to which they are subjected is of minimal use to them as education, they do want an education that fits them. Thus it is not surprising to find that the young campus chaplain often provides the forum for political action, funds for social action in the neighborhood, and facilities for the student-initiated "free university." On the other hand, I doubt that the ministers are as useful as they used to be in providing such conventional pastoral services as personal counseling, solace, or spiritual guidance. These young, the first post-Freudian generation in America, have techniques of human contact among themselves, and they are as little likely voluntarily to take their troubles to the chaplain as to the psychologist provided by the institution. Also, if the chaplain is young, he is no wiser than themselves; if he is "over 30," he is not to be trusted.

It may sound paradoxical, but a major function of a campus ministry at present is, or should be, theological. I do not mean sectarian proselytizing, which is hopeless anyway, or carrying on the traditional ritual except as a sociable and hopefully esthetic satisfaction for the diminishing number of young traditionalists. (Middle-class Jews are a special case, for their parents' guilt about not having been killed by Hitler has produced a kind of second-growth traditionalism.) In my observation, it is an error to say, like some of the writers in this book, that the present-day young are not interested in religion in a metaphysical sense. It would be odd if this were so in the transitional and revolutionary state of the present world, facing as it does a literal apocalypse. A solid agnosticism, even more than a solid faith, requires a stable world, one indeed that is on the march to a rational paradise. People might have believed this when John Dewey was a boy.

Rather, the young have been seeking in Zen, in Yoga, in love feasts with or without sex, in primitive music, in drug rituals, etc., etc., etc. They counter the discontents of civilization with a hankering for primitive experience; the complicated socialization with a desperate effort for personal communion; the complicated technology with experimental sacraments to produce instant salvation; the computer rationalism with a willingness to go crazy—temporarily. It is a rash of religiosity. And it is *intensely* intellectual—they bore you to distraction with their theories and their evidences.

Also, in our total collapse of community life, consider how like the Franciscans or the Waldenses SDS is. And the Diggers seem to go back to the Egyptian desert of the third century.

My impression is that among adolescents there is less crisis of either conversion or loss of faith than there used to be, within the traditional creeds; but there is much more religious crisis a few years later. Also, there is no definite line, sometimes no difference at all, between dissident moral and political behavior and religious feelings and experiments. The climate is somewhat like that of Dostoevski's *The Possessed*, which described a social order that was also on the skids. Chaplains who say that the students are interested in action but severely uninterested in religion should ponder the implications of the student word *commitment*.

In my opinion, the chaplains are themselves bewildered; and the more "liberal" and "modern" they have been by disposition and training, the more odd the theological scenery looks. For the "liberal" trends have not only failed to prevent but have surely furthered the catastrophic crisis of dehumanization. For instance, our present ecumenism is certainly a natural historical development of the nineteenth-century missionary movement passing into the universalist tolerance and cooperation of the League of Nations, the United Nations, One World of communications, travel, trade, and technology. But this history takes on a sinister meaning when the One World consists of Great Powers equipped with atom bombs; when the majority of mankind is growing relatively and absolutely poorer; and when Christianity has no claim to moral respect. Ecumenism then becomes either a hoax or a revolutionary political idea with unforeseeable consequences. Similarly the Social Gospel, starting in the industrial revolution and developing through the settlement houses and government welfare programs to the present war on poverty and community development, has an ambiguous ring when social work begins to look like social engineering, and when the middle class to which we want to uplift the poor is morally bankrupt. Perhaps law and order have ceased to be an option for serious Christians. And consider what has become of the century-old dialectic between the rational institutionalism of the Enlightenment, Hegel, and the Utilitarians—and the existentialism of Kierkegaard and Nietzsche. This was variously mediated by class struggle and anarchism, by personalism and psychoanalysis, by Gandhian *satyagraha*. But the dialectic falls to pieces when the rationalist pole attains its climax and theodicy is finished: specifically, if Teilhard de Chardin is right and there now exists in the world a giant spirit of communications imbued with divine love—sounding suspiciously like a universal information-retrieval computer—what is the recourse of spirit incarnate in flesh and blood except to burn the IBM card and break off the dialogue by going batty?

Admittedly, for the majority of young people today the Western tradition is quite dead. (I have spelled this out in a chapter of *Compulsory Mis-Education*.) Chaplains neither can revive it nor, in my opinion, do they *have* any doctrine to teach. But they can provide centers, and be centers, for confusion to express itself.

The Jewish Student

ALBERT HOSCHANDER FRIEDLANDER

The speaker had finished extolling Patrick Pearse and James Connolly as well as the Easter Rebellion. The strains of "Kevin Barry" filled the room. Leafing through my prayerbook, I saw that the February and October revolutions were next on the list. Following that, the reader would turn to the American scene with these words:

The CIO—formed of unskilled industrial workers in the midst of the great depression of the 1930s. The CIO was the realization of the dream of one big union. John L. Lewis led the men from the dark pits; A. Philip Randolph led the sleeping-car porters. When the miner saw the porter and each discovered that the other was black, it was the beginning of a new freedom.

And we were all to join in singing "We Shall Overcome." Then the text turned back to Europe—to the Spanish Civil War, to the Warsaw Ghetto—before returning to America and the Montgomery Bus Boycott. The congregational hymns punctuating these selections would be *"Viva la quince brigada," "Die Moorsoldaten,"* "We are moving on to Victory," and "Hold On."

The prayerbook at this unusual service was called a Haggadah; the service itself was described as a Passover Seder. The place was Columbia's Earl Hall; the time, the second evening of Passover. The congregation was made up of the members of CORE, SNCC, and other civil rights organizations on the campus. As the rabbi, I had been invited; as a person, I was a welcome guest. But the service did not relate itself to my function as a teacher of Judaism. As the organizing committee had explained to me earlier, it was a "freedom experience" to be shared by the Jewish and non-Jewish members of CORE (at a guess, about 40 per cent of those participating were not Jewish). In past years, this seder had been led by a student of Jewish background who had affiliated himself with the Quaker movement, but each year the ritual

3

was rewritten by the current membership of CORE. In some ways, this "haggadah" was curiously uninformed and naïve, and some members of the "congregation" seemed uncertain whether or not to treat the experience seriously or tongue-in-cheek. But the total atmosphere of this Freedom Seder was one of excitement and participation, of commitment and enthusiasm. There was religious fervor here, and a sense of dedication to the ethical ideas that formed the framework for the ritual. Was it Jewish? Certainly it was not the Judaism of their parents or even of most of their Jewish contemporaries on the campus. (The night before, twice their number had participated in congregational observance of Passover.) But there are those who feel this may yet be the Judaism of tomorrow: a religion almost divorced from past traditions, with a stress on secularity and upon man rather than God (with mild sarcasm, employing the jargon of the Movement, the ritual told of the Exodus: "After 300 years, a leader arose among them, and with the help of some Direct Action by God, the Jews left"), a kind of secular ecumenicism where the shared situation and ideals permit a synthesized dramatization in which the Jew functions as cultural hero and his rituals are opened to the general community—a Judaism of universalism in which the particular has been weakened to the point of extinction.

The Judaism of these students, preserving their identity to a much larger extent than previous generations of Jews on the campus, was a secularized religion. Yet it might be said that Jewish and non-Jewish students find their closest points of similarity in the patterns of secular life. For if there is an extraordinary aspect of the Jewish college student of today, it is the fact that he is quite ordinary. He is no longer kept away from the more exclusive campus by the *numerus clausus*, the old "quota system." Inequalities still do exist, but an estimated 75 per cent of college-age Jews are enrolled in schools today.

All that can be said about the student currently enrolled in the multiversity fits the Jewish students at Columbia. The general community pattern is reflected on the campus. Thus the majority of Jewish students continue to be involved with liberal causes; but they also belong to the Young Republican clubs, staff tables on the college plaza which support the war in Vietnam, and walk around with copies of Ayn Rand in their tote bag. A few of the Jewish students who perform at the Postcrypt (the campus coffee house) have added Israeli songs to their repertoire; most of their program differs little from that of other performers. They sing the civil rights and anti-war protest songs, the love ballads, the liturgies of youth in search of itself. They are the same—and yet they are different.

How does the Jewish student differ from his fellow students? Put in its simplest terms, the difference is the same as that noticed in the general community. Will Herberg's thesis of the Catholic–Protestant–Jewish pattern of American life is already in need of major revision, but the Jewish student does continue to bring a distinctly different cultural ambience into all aspects of American life—including the college campus. It might be argued that Columbia is too much encapsuled by New York and the distinctive Jewish atmosphere of that city. But a geographic-distribution admission policy has not produced significant differences in the makeup of the Jewish student group. The students from Boston, Cleveland, and Los Angeles are not too different from the New York group; and the kids from Wilkes-Barre, Little Rock, and Omaha have far more in common with their big-city friends than ever before: the mass culture which surrounds us has flattened out many of the differences and has accented common denominators. Most of them listen to the same drummer, and seldom has there been a group in American life more easy to manipulate. Yet, as we have indicated, there are differences which set the Jewish student apart: a stronger concern with ideals and causes; a greater intensity and involvement with curriculum—partially growing out of his feeling that med school and graduate studies and law school will be open only to those Jewish students who stand out in their studies. There also still seems to be a strong relationship to the family, as well as something of an identification with a Jewish cultural life and with the state of Israel, accompanied by a sense of American identity sometimes challenged by those who would raise the spurious problem of dual loyalty. Since the differences between Jew and non-Jew on the campus are not that great, it is not really proper to generalize. It is more of a personal observation, then—a suspicion rather than a statement of fact—which would make this writer suggest that there is a certain sensitivity to the tragic dimensions of life which crops up somewhat more often among the Jewish students. The American Jewish community is very much like the rest of the United States in its ignorance of the full dimension of the European catastrophe during the Hitler period. Yet there is now an influx of films, plays, and books dealing with the Holocaust. As the American temperament takes and assesses these reports dealing with God and man after Auschwitz (and Bill Hamilton, the "death-of-God" theologian, traces much of the current theological stir to a confrontation with Auschwitz), the Jewish community has had its conscious and subconscious reactions to this period of Jewish history. In some ways, behind the apparent ignorance and lack of concern with these matters, a knowledge of Jewish fate comes to the students. The observant, traditional young Jew comes to show far more concern for the fate of Russian Jewry than do his parents. The secular Jewish student tends to follow the pathway walked by Andy Goodman and Mickey Schwerner. Perhaps, in some ways, there is a reaction and an answer to the Holocaust here that can be more clearly assessed in the next decade.

There may be one other difference worth noting between the Jew and the non-Jew on campus. The Jewish community is far more tenacious in clinging to its students and demanding loyalties to its institutions. Different organizations—Orthodox, Conservative, and Reform—send their workers to the campus and strive to perpetuate the organizational differences that currently divide American life. Secular and religious, political and cultural, each of these organizations visualizes itself as the one group to which the student should relate himself in his search for identity. During the High Holydays and Passover, every major synagogue in

New York opens its doors and homes to the out-of-town students, and a major program of Sabbath home hospitality is currently developing (in sometimes competitive spirit) among these congregations. Today's major worry in American Jewish life is the threat of intermarriage, with its implications that the Jewish community has failed to hold its children. It would be unfair to ascribe today's concern with the college student to guilt feelings. Yet the almost hysterical concern about and over-emphasis on the shortcomings of today's college generation is related to this. In some ways this has been helpful. Those leaders of the Jewish community who have pleaded for years that there were more important projects to be done on the college campus are finally receiving a hearing. And the Hillel director, at one stage a stepchild of the rabbinate, is now coming into his own. But all of the turmoil and activity within the community has tended to make the Jewish student somewhat more self-conscious and aware of himself in relation to the Jewish community and to those problems of group identity with which his parents are concerned. As we turn to an examination of Jewish student life, we find that the communal pattern has been brought to the campus—but some new aspects have been added.

[2]

On the campus, as in the community, the traditional Jew is the most easily recognized Jew, a fact that has sometimes led to a distorted evaluation of his role on the campus. The fact that the traditional Jewish student community is highly vocal, cohesive, well-organized, and close to self-sufficient brings with it an overvaluation of traditionalism both within the group and on the part of the outside observer. This is quite apparent on the Columbia campus—although it must be stated from the outset that the Columbia experience is not typical of Jewish student life in the majority of American universities. The large number of Jewish undergraduates at Columbia and Barnard is atypical. Many of them are commuters, coming to Morningside Heights out of the strongholds of Jewish traditionalism: the boroughs of New York City.

What happens to the traditional student once he comes to the campus? In many cases, he ceases to be traditional. The conviction of *Torah mi-Sinai*, of the God-given Law that demands full obedience, does not stand up under the hammerings of his classes in contemporary civilization and those in philosophy. His faith in the innate superiority of the religious teachings of Orthodoxy is challenged by his fellow Jewish students at every turn. Perhaps for the first time in his life he encounters religious students who are not Orthodox and who can defend their own position with fervor and knowledge; and he finds himself surrounded by the majority of Jewish students who are comfortable in a secular Jewishness that has little to do with theological beliefs or observances.

If the traditional student moves into a dormitory, new problems assail him. With the Jewish Theological Seminary next door, it is possible to maintain a semblance of dietary observances, but it is still difficult and burdensome. The Jewish Counselor's office supports a daily *minyan* (services) and kosher Sabbath meals. But there are insidious pressures from all sides that cut into traditional rituals and observances. Since Orthodox identity quite often rests more upon observances and less upon theology, the atmosphere at the university is opposed to it: there is an openness in which almost every activity can challenge the closed Orthodox community and its observances. The student has enough self-knowledge to realize that any one discontinued ritual and observance strikes at the foundation of his Orthodoxy. More often than not, he takes this first step out of the traditional community—and the steps after that.

A sizable number stay within traditionalism. They draw close together for mutual aid and comfort, make generous and genuine sacrifices for one another, and stay in close touch with the institutions of Orthodox Jewish life in New York City. The traditional students at Columbia have developed their own program— in general as an alternate program to the Jewish program developed by other Jewish groups and by the counselors—which includes study sessions at nearby Orthodox synagogues, social gatherings open to all but attended almost exclusively by the members of Yavneh (the Orthodox college organization), and lectures in support of traditional Judaism held by outstanding thinkers such as Rabbi Soloveichik Emanuel Rackman, Rabbi Jakobovits, and others. Other lectures are given by the students themselves, particularly the graduate students on campus.

This last point is worth noting. It has been this writer's observation that the campus distinctions between the college student and the graduate scholar are far less evident in the traditionalist Jewish community on the campus. Something of a paternalism may be at work here. The Orthodox boy who is new on campus and finds his way into the Orthodox student organization is firmly taken in hand and guided into those paths where his traditionalism has the best chance of survival. Young Barnard graduates come back to campus to lead the new undergraduates in the fight for setting up more opportunities for dietary observances. And many of the graduate apartments in the vicinity serve as supplementary kitchens for young students in search of kosher food.

The emphasis on *kashrut*—dietary observances—is the chief distinguishing mark of Jewish Orthodoxy on the campus; again, it reflects what is happening in the Jewish community. To the amazement of their elders, a new and militant Orthodoxy is emerging which attacks the "laxity" of the older generation, is far less tolerant of differences, and is quite aggressive in claiming what it considers its rights within the general community. Perhaps the chief symbol of this new militancy is the *yarmulke*, the skullcap worn by traditional Jews in the synagogue when they pray. Today, the *yarmulke* is seen everywhere—on campus, in classes, in the subway, in the streets. Worn in a variety of shapes and styles, it has become the symbol of the new traditional Jew—a proud, unabashed proclamation of his Judaism. Yet there are those who worry that these outward symbols of group unity more often than not come to replace traditional dedication to the pursuit of knowledge and the sanctification of everyday life.

If there is uniformity of ritual among the Orthodox students on the college campus, this uniformity is not evident in their theology. Many of these students are not concerned with theology. Religion is not a quest for further answers, but an assured inheritance that must be safeguarded from all of the challenges of the campus. This statement in no way applies to the campus leaders. Among them, deep and sophisticated dedication to traditional Jewish thought finds reinforcement from contemporary philosophies. The existentialist traditionalism of Joseph Soloveitchik, who gave a three-hour lecture not long ago on the campus, has left its mark; and most of these students have read the Rav's great article on "The Lonely Man of Faith" published in 1965. But alongside these students, who represent the best of traditional Jewish thought, there does exist that large number who reject nontraditional Judaism and the outside world with an uninformed fanaticism that seems strange on the Columbia campus.

There is, then, no easy way to summarize the traditional Jewish student on the campus. Any generalization would tend to obscure the diversity of thought and action that fits under the mantle of Orthodoxy. All we can do is report what happens on this particular campus and try to assess how these observations fit into the general pattern of student life and of religion on the campus. Nevertheless, it is clear that Orthodoxy is very much alive; traditional Judaism has firmly established itself upon the campus, and the identity of the Orthodox student is much more apparent to him and to his peers than that of any other group on campus.

For the Jew who has remained Orthodox, the problems of self-identification seem to have been solved. He brings his identity with him to the campus. Sociologically and psychologically he remains much more than the others a member of his family, carrying with him an environment which surrounds him as a protective wall. He does not reach out for the new values the educative process is to bring to him; rather, he tests the new knowledge against the established standards upon which his existence is founded. And it may be said that, by his very presence, he makes a valid contribution to the campus: in his self-assured identity as a traditional Jew, he presents the academic community an authentic Jewish existence that cannot be ignored. The campus cannot accept his own definition that it is the only authentic Jewish existence possible. But it must come to terms with the traditional position and show that there are, indeed, real alternatives to it.

[3]

The traditionalist Jew tends to preempt the term *religious* for himself. The majority of Jewish students, who think of themselves as Jewish but not as religious, are willing to grant this claim of traditionalism. But there is a sizable group, recruited from left-wing Conservative Judaism (right-wing Conservative Judaism has pretty much accepted Orthodox standards and is now striving to overcome its own institutional history in an effort to find acceptance among the traditionalists) and from the Reform Jewish movement, which identifies itself as both Jewish and religious. To the extent that this group is organized, the leadership comes from students who have graduated from the youth organizations of institutional Judaism: the National Federation of Temple Youth and the United Synagogue Youth. Religious services are important to them, but do not take precedence over everything else. Services are conducted every two weeks, and an earlier tendency to rewrite the prayerbook has given way to a standardized use of the Conservative prayerbook supplemented by English readings and treated so that the resultant service is closer to Reform than to mainline Conservatism. The service is preceded by a Sabbath dinner—held at the same time and in the same building as the Orthodox Sabbath dinner.

The differences between the two "religious" groupings become evident here. Both meals are kosher, are prepared by the same students (under the close supervision of traditionalists), and are then brought into separate rooms. All attempts to fuse these groups into one have failed. In part this is due to the fact that the traditionalists cannot surrender any of their ceremonies—be it the ritual washing of hands between the sanctification over the

wine and blessing over the bread or the long grace after meals—
and feel that their non-Orthodox friends should be instructed and
elevated by this. The Conservative-Liberal group feels threatened
in its own identity, in its right to maintain a greatly modified
ritual which need not be followed rigidly but which may not be
dismissed as insufficient. Also, both groups know different songs
and use different melodies for the same songs; and these songs—
when the groups met together—came to emphasize rivalries and
in-group feelings. In the end, the institutional split so evident in
all of American Jewish life also manifests itself on the college
campus. And, in the students' minds, a sharp distinction is made
between Yavneh, the Orthodox student organization (the traditional Sabbath meals are not organized by Yavneh but by a
student group working independently with the Jewish counselors, but many of the participants refer to these meals as the
Yavneh dinners) and Seixas-Menorah, the over-all campus organization, which is considered nontraditional. The Seixas-Menorah
discussion groups are attended by the Conservative-Liberal
group. But, in contrast to the life of the Orthodox group, there
are few social events. Unburdened by the fear of intermarriage
which haunts their parents, these students find that the social
events of a campus which is some 50 per cent Jewish more than
serves their needs. Living in full openness and in friendliness
towards his neighbor, the Orthodox student who does not surrender his Orthodoxy lives apart from the rest of the campus
community. The Conservative and Reform Jewish student,
whether or not he accents the religious nature of his Judaism,
lives in the midst of the university.

The "religious" student goes against the main currents of
campus life. Both students and administration treat him with
respect and consideration. This consideration, though, is directed
more toward the free practice of religious rituals and customs
visible in the life of the Orthodox student. (Christian traditionalists, incidentally, are somewhat puzzled by their encounters
with students who place heavy ritual obligations on their daily
life but feel no need or desire to explore theological problems.)

The nontraditional Jewish student who affirms religious convictions and maintains these in the framework of a life that shows no outward differences from that of his neighbor is likely to encounter much more opposition. He has taken an intellectual position opposed by his peers, one not safeguarded by his own observances, as an aspect of his individuality that is to be respected. By going beyond the claim of his cultural Jewishness—which both Jews and non-Jews concede in a number of interesting ways to be discussed later—to the espousing of Judaism, he has placed himself in a difficult position. Will he defend the institutions of the adult community, the Jewish "Establishment"—whether Orthodox, Conservative, or Reform? The reaction of the campus against the Establishment is almost unanimous. Even those who know that they are being trained to take their place in that Establishment, and who enjoy both the training and the knowledge of what their future will be, like to play at being rebels: a mild rebellion is the conformists' way of coping with a situation where nonconformity is the norm. Indeed, today's arrival of the radical student and the concept of the "free university" is the recognition that this kind of "campus rebellion" is artificial, a final playtime that is not to threaten the *status quo*.

The nontraditional Jewish student who sees himself as religious does not defend the Establishment. Like the majority of Jewish students, he sees the American synagogue as the place of conspicuous consumption where the Bar Mitzvah ceremonies are more and more lavish, where the High Holyday services are a fashion parade of *haute couture* and mink, and where the rabbi takes his text from Walter Lippmann and *The New York Times*. He can and does identify himself with the increasing emphasis on social justice that has established local and international work projects for the synagogue youth of the Reform movement and has brought the younger rabbis to Alabama and Mississippi. But the basic stance he takes is that of an individual who draws out of a religious tradition that was never exclusively identified with the synagogue or other communal institutions but rises out of the everyday situation in which all things have an aspect of holiness and nothing has become sacred to the extent of being removed from life. Judaism has always been a layman's religion. Its cultural inheritance has kept it from being completely submerged by the materialistic and secular forces found in today's American scene. There has been an apprehension of the mystery, of the transcendental beyond the phenomenal; and there has been the constantly stressed awareness of the moral action that takes precedence above all else. The liberal Jewish student who affirms his religion must stress both mystery and commandment for himself where the more secular student immersed in the Jewish tradition gives assent to those ethical imperatives that may come to him as much out of the general as from the specific Jewish heritage.

In talking to the students who want to speak for a liberal religion on the campus scene, one is struck with the unanimity they display in rejecting the religious Establishment. Much as they have been influenced by young rabbis to whom they still feel close, they do not see these men as a source of religious authority. They appreciate the religious literature of Judaism, and find it instructive and necessary for their religious development. But, again, they will not refer to this as the basis for belief. It is neither an argument they can address to their peers nor a reality of faith into which they can enter freely. Instead, they turn inward. The ontological self-search espoused by Tillich in the Christian community is evident in this area of Jewish life. And these students have come to a personal encounter with the mystery within their own existence before they relate it to their religious heritage. At that point, they abandon much of the religious language of their fathers; the area of the sacred has to be redefined, and the religion itself has to be taken out of the cultural structure and has to be placed into prophetic confrontation with that society. But at that point, with a highly personal religion drawn out of a polarity of sacred and secular realms of being, one is hard put to distinguish the unaffiliated liberal religious young Jew from the secular Jewish student.

[4]

The distinction between the "secular" and the "religious" Jewish student is actually unrealistic once the traditionalist notion of what constitutes religion is put aside. Where there are no creeds to recite, no sure test of faith, no distinctive observances to proclaim Judaism, the basic standard that remains for the Jewish faith is the ethical act. Much soul-searching has gone on among the Jewish leadership with regard to the thousands of civil rights workers who come from a Jewish background but have only the most tenuous links to their religion. In the end, the community has been proud to include them in its definition of what truly constitutes a religious Jew. Yet by their own definition, based upon their image of a calcified and materialistic Establishment of Judaism in America, many of these students would reject the definition. Where they believe in ideology, they strive for a universalism unalloyed by particularism. Where ideology is rejected, they feel themselves in opposition to the realities of the American Jewish scene.

One of my rabbinic colleagues found himself jailed in Mississippi with a fellow civil rights worker who claimed he was not Jewish. A lengthy discussion between them culminated in the discovery that he was not only Jewish but a distant cousin of the rabbi. In the same way, walking inside the Selma compound behind the wall, I was accosted by a number of students simply because I wore a *yarmulke* and thus proclaimed myself a rabbi. The approach was almost always the same: "Rabbi, I haven't talked to a rabbi or attended a service in years. I simply could not go into those mausoleums they call temples, those Bar Mitzvah factories. But when I see a rabbi here in Selma, alongside me, I can talk to him. And I want to talk to him."

The Freedom Seder mentioned at the beginning comes into perspective here. There is a religious need, a religious reaching toward expression for many of the students involved in civil rights and anti-war activities. That need is not necessarily filled by the clergymen who participate in the Movement. More often than not, these clergymen are coolly exploited and utilized by the movement, which was quick to recognize that the Establishment had handed them a tool that could be used to great advantage. For most ministers involved in these activities are liberals, not radicals. As Henry Malcom has rightly pointed out, the current confrontation in the movement pits the radicals against the liberals; and few rabbis could accept the radical ideology or techniques. Yet if the movement's leadership is more and more taken from among the radical wing, the college students involved continue to be drawn in large measure from liberalism. And many of the rabbis involved feel it not unreasonable to hope that these students may yet return to the synagogues and give them new content and meaning. While some of the older rabbis view such phenomena as the Freedom Seder and fok-song sessions with dismay and perturbation, I feel obligated to stress their positive aspects. Bill Starr has properly pointed to the new liturgy (i.e., the fok song) and new student groupings as the place for religious expression. And the observations made by the other writers in this study can most certainly be applied to the Jewish student on the Columbia campus in view of the percentages involved.

There are radical and liberal Jewish students who help define Judaism on the campus. There are the traditional students, religious students from Reform and Conservative backgrounds, and students whose primary Jewish interest is Zionism: all of them lend color and variety to this Jewish scene. It must be noted, incidentally, that the Zionist group is small, poorly organized, and not a force on campus. Once Zionism was a passionate cause attracting many; now it is a private devotion for a small group of dedicated individuals who struggle against student apathy in their effort to relate the Israeli scene to the campus. They are not alone in this struggle against apathy. At Columbia —typical of the multiversity—the cool and uninvolved student is in the majority. Where the sensation-hunter sees flaming rebellion and discontent on the campus, and where the educator hopes for a community of scholars engaged in the search for truth, the dispassionate observer is more likely to find a comfortable and somewhat sluggish group of students who are well paid by their parents as they prepare themselves to take on roles in their fathers' business or in law, medicine, or education. The Jewish student, more often than not, is running scared. He fights for top grades, he takes "gut" courses, he uses the summers for extra preparation. But he knows that he has a good chance to make it big in the outside world, and education is all too often used as only a means to a materialistic end. And the many students who delight in the intellectual adventure are also fully aware that government subsidies and fellowships can extend their sojourn in the groves of academe to decades. The Jewish community has always prized scholarship: "My son the professor" does not sound bad after law and medicine have been ruled out. But the familiar term *Der ewige Student*—the eternal student—has those undertones of disapproval Jewish life directs against those who would always remain in preparation for the task and never enter upon it. The eternal graduate student is part of university life today. But, on the whole, it should be said that the involvement with study (perhaps more evident within the Jewish student group than outside it) is a positive one. And this world of the Jewish student, which we have approached through some of the types that are recognizable, is in truth a world: filled with individuality; unpredictable, very much alive; in search of meaning; achieving much for which we look in vain outside the university. There is a greater openness to student life—the Jewish student is more likely to trust his neighbor and to consider him a friend and not a rival. Even in the cool world of noncommitment there are ideals and hopes for the future. And religious messianism—apocalyptic or not—will always find itself at home in the university pattern where the growth of knowledge is presumed to enrich and to enlarge the present and the future.

[5]

The typology of individual Jewish students may give us some insights into what is happening on the college scene. Nevertheless, the over-all picture is far too complex to respond to this treatment. If there is a new Judaism on the new campus of today, it is not found within any one type, but rather in the campus situation itself. Student concerns, the teaching of religion in the framework of the university, the specific function of rabbi and minister on campus—all these come together and must be seen as one configuration before a general statement about campus religion is possible. It may therefore be worthwhile to turn to a specific campus event in which these component parts found some expression and to relate this incident to our present analysis.

Rolf Hochhuth, author of the controversial play *The Deputy*, which questioned the Pope's rôle in the death of six million Jews, came to the Columbia campus the week before his play opened on Broadway (March 1964). There was only a one-day advance notice of his arrival. No advance publicity was given his visit; and university identification cards were required for admission to the Barnard gymnasium, with police guards at the door. Yet more than an hour before his scheduled appearance, more than twelve hundred students had filled the gymnasium; a large number of would-be listeners were turned away.

There was no picketing, and there were no disturbances outside the building. Inside, the overflow crowd filled the balcony, bleachers, and floor space facing the stage. On stage, name cards along a table indicated the participants of the panel that was to join Mr. Hochhuth: Professors Eric Bentley, Fritz Stern, and Rabbi Albert Friedlander of Columbia University; Professor Tom Driver of Union Theological Seminary and drama critic for *The Reporter;* Hans Holthusen, director of the Goethe Haus; and Mr. Becker and Professor Bauke of Columbia's German Department, who chaired the meeting and served as interpreters for Mr. Hochhuth. A number of Catholic spokesmen had been invited; none could attend.

Professor Stern began the proceedings with some historical observations, received a little impatiently by the students. But they warmed up when Eric Bentley, an old campus favorite, spoke with verve and humor: the play had flaws—it had not been translated by Eric Bentley! But it contained a powerful message of three silences that had taken place while the smoke of Belsen filled the skies. Mankind had been silent. The Pope had been silent. And God had been silent. That last silence, concluded Bentley, had been the worst of all. Professor Driver concurred with Bentley. It was the terrible silence of God that sounds out of that history and out of the play.

Yet not all of Dr. Driver's anger was directed against God. Some of it was reserved for the New York producers who succeeded in "making the play a colossal bore"; for that he could not forgive them. All of these comments had been translated for Mr. Hochhuth, who answered in German, with a subsequent translation by Mr. Becker for most of the audience.

In defense of God, Mr. Hochhuth quoted Martin Buber: "One cannot talk about God; one can only talk to God." True enough, the last act in his written play had been addressed to God (*"Die Frage nach Gott"*); but the basic issue in the play had been the silence of the Pope. In defense of the producers, Mr. Shumlin and Mr. Kolitz, he pointed out the difficulties of reducing a seven-hour play to one of less than three hours. But he also felt that some scenes—notably the one dealing with the deporting of the Jewish family in Rome—should be restored; and he felt that the character of Jacobson had been changed for the worse.

As the rabbi on the panel, this writer was then asked for his comments. The student newspapers noted that the rabbi was most impressed (and depressed) by the silence of the German people and by the fact that the play "was not centered on the silence of God, but on the silence of man. Guilt cannot be placed outside our existence"—an indication of the conflict between the rabbi and other panelists. Nihilism and neo-Orthodoxy merge at the point at which responsibility is placed on the cosmic level; in either case, human guilt is emptied of meaning. It becomes too vast or it is placed with God. The central point of the play—that man is committed to action in the face of evil, that inaction is a denial of human responsibility—seemed obscured by an emphasis on the silence of God that blanketed the silence of men. Both the audience and Mr. Hochhuth seemed to concur in this; and it brought the discussion back to the play itself.

Questions from the students (written on cards and translated for Mr. Hochhuth) now came to the panel. Some dealt with the protagonists of the play: Kurt Gerstein, the true Protestant, who made a pact with the devil to save lives, who entered the SS and played a dangerous double game until he died. An interesting question was raised by Mr. Holthusen: "Why does Gerstein, after his personality had been fully developed and integrated into the play, disappear midway through the action?" Hochhuth's answer was simple and true: "That is the way of life; more than that, it is what happened."

At the same time, Hochhuth confessed that Piscator (the Berlin director) had raised the same question, and that Hochhuth had reintroduced Gerstein into the last scene of the written play—a piece of writing he regretted now. What of the concentration-camp doctor? . . . Was he not a figure of almost mythological evil . . . a surrealist form unrelated to the rest of the cast? The author agreed; evil Germany *had* taken on mythological proportions; the doctor was intended to stand out from the other characters in his uniqueness. On the other hand, characters like the Nazi corporal in his straightforward brutality and the Italian fascist in his weak viciousness stood for the bulk who followed a multitude to do evil.

The core of the play is the condemnation of the Pope. Here Hochhuth was adamant. The cadences of Martin Luther's high hopes and bitter disappointments with regard to Rome sounded out of Hochhuth's voice: "I challenge the position of the Pope because he was the person who had the highest moral obligation. He was also that person who even in material and social matters had the greatest influence." Against all questions and challenges raised by students, Hochhuth maintained that the Pope, as God's deputy, had to speak out against the evil of Hitler's concentration camps. Three years of research had convinced the author that the Pope's silence condemned Jews to death, that the voice of the

Vatican would have slowed the work of extermination to some extent, and that Pius XII had to be called to account for his silence.

This did not mitigate the sin of Germany: "The failure of the fire brigade does not make the arsonist less guilty." Indeed, the great second scene in the book (the beer-hall sequence) shows all aspects of German society, from the industrialists to the intellectuals, in the full guilt of their involvement. But when the producers cut out all of these portions and concentrated on the charge against the Pope, they were true to Hochhuth's purpose. The play is *not* anti-Catholic: Riccardo Fontana represents the true Catholic in all his integrity. It is *not* anti-Vatican-family. It *is* anti-Pope Pius XII—against this particular person and his specific actions.

Some strange questions were sent up from the floor, written by students who seemed far away from the reality of the Hitler period. One letter (not read in public) came from "an Orthodox Jew" to enlighten Professor Bentley on the nature of God's silence: "We don't question God's attempt to teach his world a lesson. I pray that, perhaps, we have learned something." The student who wrote this note was a freshman. Perhaps, in time, he will learn something.

One question that was read addressed itself to the rabbi: "Why did the Jews depend on people of other religions to fight and shelter them—why did the Jews not defend themselves; for example, like the French Resistance?" The answer to this question took some time. It tried to sketch the heroism of Jewish life that the student might understand, from the Warsaw Ghetto to the concentration-camp uprisings, the heroism of the individual and of the group; it tried to sketch the full historic situation, so that the student might see how ignorance can become almost blasphemy; and it tried to sketch the heroism of Jewish life that the student might never understand: acts of prayer, acts of study, acts of love in the face of inevitable death—a heroism not based on strength, or on power, but on God's spirit. Many students did understand, as their loud and sustained applause indicated.

The panelists—Mr. Hochhuth in particular—associated themselves with this statement. At the same time, Mr. Hochhuth was careful not to become embroiled in what may have seemed to be an internal Jewish problem. When a student asked him to comment on Hannah Arendt's *Eichmann in Jerusalem*, his answer was somewhat as follows: "The basic importance of this book lies in the fact that it reminds the world of the sins that were committed by the Nazis. I cannot judge the validity of some of her criticisms, but I, and the German people, can be challenged to the same severe self-examination of our past that we find in this book."

The meeting ended shortly after this, and Mr. Hochhuth left the campus. But the issues he had raised remained with the students and were heatedly discussed in the next days. One side issue was resolved: the changes made in the portrayal of Jacobson. Zvi Kolitz, coproducer of *The Deputy*, addressed a Jewish student meeting five days later. "Mr. Hochhuth has not met many Jews and does not understand the Jew fully," he said. "In the original play, Jacobson is shown swearing vengeance against the Germans when he discovers that his parents have been killed in Auschwitz. But we felt that the Jacobson we know would not have made the issue one of family vendetta. It is the death of the Jewish people and not the death of his parents that has Jacobson in its grasp; and when he promises that he will return as the avenger he speaks for all of Israel."

It was in the figure of Jacobson that many Jewish students seemed to discover themselves. In their confrontation with Hochhuth, they had come to see *The Deputy* as a morality play in which each character became a symbol invested with special meaning: Gerstein was the good Protestant; Father Riccardo was the good Catholic; the Doctor was evil itself; the Pope the symbol of indifference; and Jacobson was the Jew. They shared his passion and his need for vengeance.

It is unlikely that such was Hochhuth's intent. Consciously or not, he had cast the Jew in another role. With all of its realism, the written play centers upon two symbolic actions: the Pope washes his hands and declares that he is innocent; Riccardo accepts the star of David from Jacobson and pins it upon his own breast. With that action his fate is sealed: he has become the scapegoat who must die for the sins of the world, the scapegoat who is identical with Jacob-Israel. The Jewish star is the cross he must bear (and in Jacobson there appears the one who was crucified).

The star of David has become the Star of Redemption, and Franz Rosenzweig's vision leaves the realm of the metahistorical and enters the world of experience in a Christian statement of revelation and redemption.

[6]

This confrontation between Hochhuth and the Columbia students is highly important because it gives us the opportunity to study the reactions of the group and of the individuals. The framework of the encounter is the Holocaust with its questions to the Jew and non-Jew of the post-Auschwitz world. The answer by the Orthodox student (at least in this instance and for this person) showed an inability to deal with this question. In the same way, a number of Jewish students echoed the confusion of that segment of the Jewish community which has accepted the idea that the victims contributed to their deaths through their passivity. A misstatement of the historical situation, this analysis still takes hold of students who have increasingly become aware of their own helplessness vis-à-vis the society around them. For those Jewish students who have identified themselves with their people and culture but not with their religion, the past must be rehabilitated and fitted into a pattern upon which they may build. Thus is created an artificial history that fails in its task because the general is made to appear as the particular.

But the chief question of Hochhuth's play reaches out to everyone: How could this happen? The secularist is asked: How could man be silent and be an accomplice in this crime through his inaction? The religionist is bluntly asked: How could God be silent? How could he permit this to happen? For many, from the Reverend William Hamilton down to the student who wrote Nietzsche's word about the demise of God on the wall of the 116th Street subway station, the only answer dealing adequately with the world of Auschwitz and Bergen-Belsen was the word that "God is dead." One of the dangers contained in this answer, as already suggested, is that the silence of God casts a concealing shade over the silence of man. But the man of religion, whether student or rabbi, who wants to meet this challenge to his faith, must be aware that the student on campus (or the man in the city) will not any longer accept the "tried and true" answers of religion.

Job's comforters saw suffering as an ennobling experience with which God purged man's shortcomings. But how does this apply to the radiation-torn survivors of Hiroshima, to the little children who left their shoes and overcoats outside the gas chambers, to a quarter-million Indonesians murdered in one bloody week of terror? The traditional concept of God's justice falls short at this point.

Nor is the mystic's faith liable to win acceptance on the campus. The *deus absconditus*, the hidden God—who is sometimes far and sometimes near, who speaks at times and is silent at other times—cannot be taken from the man of faith, but he is irrelevant to the student in search of answers to the tragic nature of our century. Nevertheless, there is something in the mystic's world that reaches out to the campus. It could almost be said that Christianity discovered Martin Buber before the Jewish community came to terms with him. But there are Jewish students who are now reading Buber's *Eclipse of God* and *I and Thou* for the first time, and who see in Buber a breakthrough in both theology and epistemology. Some students—very few, really—have ventured in and out of the world of Zen, which seems to have had its run. Yet one cannot but wonder whether LSD may not influence student thinking in the years ahead—particularly if it becomes relatively safe to "take that trip." Campus Judaism does not seem to be headed in that direction. But many of the fine minds among both students and faculty do move in the direction of religious existentialism: where the Jewish religionist finds himself opposed to the dreadful freedom of Sartre's existentialism, he can and does feel an authentic Judaism in the teachings of Martin Buber and his followers. And it is clearly evident that the Jewish community on and off the campus, shaken to the roots of its own existence by the Holocaust, is in search of a faith that will give meaning to the asking of ultimate questions even when it cannot give full answers.

[7]

What is the function of the rabbi, his purpose on campus? In the Columbia pattern that has been described in these pages, the clergyman's role has been defined in a number of ways: he is an advisor and counselor who deals with the specific problems of the college student and places these problems into a larger frame of reference. He teaches any number of noncredit courses dealing with the culture, the theology, and the rituals of his religion. He stands between administration and student and must be true to both of them. He runs coffee houses, marches against the war in Vietnam, supports civil rights groups, organizes social events and protest meetings, and lectures in the dorms on sexual morality. With his fellow ministers he walks around as a living example of ecumenicity. He gives invocations to the alumni society and says a kind word to the downtrodden Lions after the football game. He has tea with the deans and cider with the students. And nothing he does has any meaning if he is not a man of God.

Sometimes a clergyman, rabbi or not, balks at this designation. He is not sure the association is a credible one in the sight of the students. He would rather be known as a man among men, who speaks for himself alone.

But does he speak for himself alone? He may go tripping with the students; he may be the foremost exponent of the "new morality" on campus; there may be channels of communication between him and the students unavailable to many of his colleagues—but the initial point of contact between him and them is still the fact that he is "a man of God." He is on campus for a purpose. And his relationship to the whole university community cannot be channeled toward one group alone. For there are still those students who come to rabbi, priest, or minister because they see him as a religious figure—and often as a figure of authority—not because the rabbi is one of the boys. At this point, new language and new insights are needed—above all, the rabbi has to communicate, has to show a concern for the student, for the student's problem, *not* for the institution. But he acts with the knowledge that the "sacred realm" of institutional religion has been rejected by the mainstream of Jewish tradition—that from the time of the Pharisees, the task of the rabbi has been the sanctification of the secular, a daily existence.

The campus minister who only represents his institution is a menace on campus. At almost any university one may find religious figures of authority who are blindly and fanatically devoted to the "ancient, unchanging values and institutions." Almost intentionally they alienate the student. "We live in the new Dark Ages," they tell one another, "and we must preserve the true faith and the true institution. Let all but the few, the faithful, leave this structure! Eventually, the Sea of Faith will flood back into the sanctuary which we guard for the future." These are guardians of a dead past, and I cannot see that they will have a share in the future.

There is a new rabbi on the campus today, one who can and does address himself to the new needs of the student. The form of his religious commitment differs from place to place. A Richard Israel at Yale is "Orthoprax" in many ways, informed by Hassidic thought as much as by the Reform seminary that ordained him. Richard Rubinstein at Pittsburgh blends the *En Soph* of the Zohar with the dreadful nothingness of existentialism. Other campus rabbis have built upon the new thinking which came from the German Jewish community's flowering before the Holocaust: they speak in terms of Martin Buber, Franz Rosenzweig, and Leo Baeck. All of them, to a greater extent than their colleagues in congregations, keep up with the new worlds of cybernetics and analytical thinking. Nevertheless, they do not teach their private or their public theology: they teach themselves. The student at Columbia (in contrast, let us say, to an undergraduate at Cambridge or Oxford, where ideology is much more discussed) asks the pragmatic questions of his environment: what the rabbi thinks is far less important than what he does. Dick Israel and Rabbi Rubinstein, to return to these men as examples, have both led their students into civil rights forays.

The rabbi who is involved, who cares, who enters the student's life with full concern, who refuses to be the policeman for the parents but becomes the genuine spokesman of student needs ultimately fulfills his religious function. For he teaches the basis of Judaism: the inestimable value of the individual in which the Divine is encountered.

The Changing Campus Scene:
From Church to Coffeehouse

WILLIAM F. STARR

Traditional Western theology has tended to identify with the *status quo*. It has seen meaning in order rather than in change, and has tended to condemn all thought of change as if the dynamic process of change were a threat. For centuries the church has identified, and has been identified, with law and order rather than forces for change and freedom. James Russell Lowell chides the church in his splendid heretical poem and hymn-lyric "Once to Every Man and Nation," in which he points to

> Some great cause, God's new Messiah,
> Off'ring each the bloom or blight,
> And the choice goes by for ever
> 'Twixt that darkness and that light.
>
> New occasions teach new duties,
> Time makes ancient good uncouth;
> They must upward still and onward
> Who would keep abreast of truth.

This verse presages the mood of what mass media have popularized as "the New Theology." Like the "rugged individualist" creed of the nineteenth century, the New Theology maintains a confident openness to the future and a willingness to dispense with goods which have become "uncouth."

Just as the New Theology is re-examining the traditional doctrines and teachings of the church, so the university campus of today is seeking to understand its place in a rapidly changing world. We might say that the mood of both New Theology and "New Campus" is radical in the classical sense of the word—that root questions are being asked, that the deepest foundations are being called upon to justify their continued existence. One rather disturbed spectator at a worship service that featured a sermon on the death of God asked in exasperation, "Is nothing sacred?"

The preacher retorted smilingly, "Not any more, Madam, not any more." Yet in a deeper sense the questions that are being asked are a guarantee that the mantle of sacredness will not be bestowed simply as a reward for staying power. Perhaps the passion of today's college students for honesty, and their impatience with forms whose content is lost, will lead to a fresh, authentic discovery of sacredness in the midst of life.

We are witnessing a struggle between the university's quest for freedom and society's concern for order and stability. Students and faculty alike tend to reject the doctrine that truth is to be found by a ritualistic study of the legacy of the past. It is no accident that the academic life is often described by such adjectives as *dry, tedious, mechanical,* and *trivial.* The student of today is willing to play this game, but his actions often echo the existential protest against this kind of pursuit for the truth. The quest for freedom and truth on today's campus echoes Kierkegaard's dictum: "Truth is the truth which builds you up [which edifies] . . . truth . . .[is] truth *for thee.*"

This pursuit of truth has been the *raison d'être* of the university since its beginnings at the end of the twelfth century. The word itself is made up of two Latin words which mean "to combine into one." Through the ages *universitas* has referred to both a sociological and an intellectual combining-into-one. A working definition of a university, then, is a community of persons associated for the rational pursuit of truth. But this definition raises more questions than it answers because it begs the questions of the terms used: What is a community? What is a person? What do we mean by rational? What do we mean by pursuit here? With Pilate we must ask, "What is truth?"

It is no accident that these questions are also the questions being asked by our culture, by our world. Insofar as the university is a microcosm of culture it reflects and articulates such questions; it also reflects the attempt of culture to find answers to the questions raised by its own existence.

The university of today is an institution in the midst of "revolution." We could even say that the university *is* a revolution that at the same time reflects the social, moral, scientific, and humanistic revolutions it helps inspire. The word *university* conjures up images of rapid growth—new buildings, ever greater numbers of students, faculty, areas of study, research facilities and materials. To speak of university is to speak of growth and of change.

It is apparent, however, that the university itself is ambivalent about its role as incubator for rapid change. Although it recognizes that constant change is one of the basic facts of its existence, at the same time the university harbors those who view the constant shifting of center, the eloquent testimony of the great power of change in our world, with suspicion, distrust, and at times with outright hostility. The conservative spirit—the desire to conserve and preserve the legacy of the past—is often embodied in the administration and trustees of our universities.

Bishop John Robinson, one of the popularizers of the New Theology, examines the tension that must always exist "between the fixed and the free, the constant and the changing, the absolute and the relative." He suggests that "we need not fear flux: God is in the rapids as much as in the rocks, and as Christians we are free to swim and not merely to cling." The New Theology urges us to cast out over 20,000 fathoms and swim for it; clinging may give one a sense of security in the midst of change, but in the end it leads to exhaustion and futility. The New Theology recognizes that a revolution in thought and action has already taken place in the world. Its task is to try to discern what response the Christian can make to what Kenneth Boulding calls "the post-civilized world."

Three aspects of what I am calling the New Theology illuminate present-day styles of campus ministry: first, they offer new understandings about God, including the so-called death-of-God theologies; second, they give current thoughts about the Church; third, they afford a new look at Jesus, who is called the Christ.

A New Understanding of God

In *Honest to God*, which created a sensation in ecclesiastical circles in 1963, Bishop John Robinson opens the Pandora's box of theology by asking radical questions about the traditional language and substance of the Christian faith. As a Bishop of the Anglican Church, Robinson is keenly aware of his role as "defender of the faith" (*defensor fide*); at the same time he contends that much more is required than a simple restating of traditional orthodoxy in modern terms: a radical recasting is demanded, "in the process of which the most fundamental categories of our theologies—of God, of the supernatural, and of religion itself—must go into the melting."

The first area of concern in the New Theology is language. Robinson focuses upon the problem of using pictorial language to represent and describe spiritual realities. Death-of-God theologians like William Hamilton are more concerned with the tone of theological language, with finding the right way to speak the truth to another. Although these two theologians approach the problem from different points of view, each in his way is pointing to a crisis in communication which is a hallmark of the twentieth century.

Both theologians and secular writers (novelists, poets, dramatists) speak of the inadequacy of traditional God-language as a way of expressing their own experiences and convictions and, more important, as a means of conducting a significant conversation with "the world." The reluctance of many New Theologians to preach the faith in the usual stentorian tones is rooted in their concern with how we talk with one another. This has been a theme of nontheological writing for some time.

In *The New Essence of Christianity*, William Hamilton suggests that the tone of our speech, the way in which what we see and believe is spoken, is as important as the structure and form of what we say. He sees an analogy between the diminishing range and confidence of such modern novelists as Albert Camus and Ignazio Silone in Europe and Faulkner and Hemingway in this country (in contrast to the confident range and sweep of James Joyce and Thomas Mann) and his own unwillingness to make strident, confident pronouncements about God. In the new generation of novelists we find "a retreat to the knowable, the polishing and perfecting of the little that is known, the careful attempt not to write and to say everything in large and confident tones."

Paul Tillich suggests that the artistic realm is the most sensitive barometer for the spiritual climate of any age. A brief look at contemporary writers' concern for language makes this abundantly clear. In *Burnt Norton*, T. S. Eliot wrote:

> Words strain,
> Crack and sometimes break, under the burden,
> Under the tension, slip, slide, perish,
> Decay with imprecision, will not stay in place,
> Will not stay still. Shrieking voices
> Scolding, mocking, or merely chattering,
> Always assail them.

Eliot, to be sure, is speaking of the perennial frailty of language. Emotions experienced, ideas conceived, convictions rooted in the depths of one's being are not easy to put into words. Yet at the same time he is speaking of one of the curses and crises accented in our age—the inability really to speak to one another. He is saying that this is partly due to the noisy, scolding, mocking, chattering voices of our world. Man feels "over-against" others as he tries to communicate with them.

The members of Captain Ahab's crew in *Moby Dick* were described as "nearly all islanders, [none] acknowledging the common continent of men, but each . . . living on a continent of his own." The urban dweller of today qualifies for this crew. He huddles in a great asphalt jungle, painfully aware of its emptiness. He has lost the sense of nearness to friends and neighbors. Although he lives closer and closer to them in great urban fortresses, he finds it harder and harder to recognize his fellows or to hold onto a sense of his own identity. This is a world from which the gracious marks of "presence" have been banished.

Literary critic Nathan Scott interprets the banishment of these marks of presence in the light of an insight of Karl Jaspers. Jaspers draws an analogy between primitive man and man of today. Just as primitive man believed that he stood face to face with demons and believed that if he could but know their names he could become their master, so contemporary man is faced by something, or someone, incomprehensible, which disorders his calculations. "The nameless powers of Nothingness," Jaspers tells us, "are, in our world whence the Gods have been driven forth, the analogy of the demons that confronted primitive man."

The nameless powers of nothingness: another way of saying that the old God-hypothesis—the old assumption that God must be in his heaven because all is right with the world—is no longer believable or understandable. The forces that tear us apart and separate us and disorder our lives are most real to us—not the powers of harmony and order, of loving-kindness and understanding that used to be attributed to God. These disruptive forces are the nameless powers of nothingness because they have their origin in loss and emptiness and estrangement and despair.

If we accept the sensitivity of writers of our time to the spiritual predicament of modern man, then we can understand why he has lost the ability to talk about God; indeed, he has lost the sense of God's presence in the world. This is one reason for the belief that God is silent, and absent, and even dead. Because man has not lived in real nearness to others, he has not known the gracious reality of presence in relationship, and so his imagination has been unable to grasp the possibility of the world itself being grounded in a transcendent Presence. He cannot talk about God because that sense of nearness which makes us able to speak has not been a part of his life.

Paul Tillich suggests that when the First World War broke out the sense of loneliness and exile which had already been expressed by such writers as Dostoevski, Baudelaire, and Kafka became the dominant experience of the age. Mankind has suffered a trauma, a radical dislocation. He has lost the sense of confidence in history. Everything might not turn out all right. James Joyce speaks of history as a nightmare from which he is trying to awake.

What one feels in so much contemporary thought is a deep need for the restoration of trust in the stoutness and reliability and essential healthiness of earthly things. Contemporary novelists and theological writers have moved away from the cosmic concerns of such giants as James Joyce, Franz Kafka, and Thomas Mann; they have withdrawn to the knowable. The dislocation and tragic sense of loss of 1914 no longer evoke anguished cries and sweeping claims about man and his world. For the writer of today it is but a sad memory. His concern is to say as much as he feels he can say about what he sees and feels and knows and longs for. In so doing he finds meaning in the earthly things, and people, around him.

The challenge to find meaning in this world without appealing to cosmic benevolence or eternal verities is being met by writers like Albert Camus and Ignazio Silone and by theological writers like Dietrich Bonhoeffer, John Robinson, and William Hamilton. Once the shock of the statement "God is dead" has abated they are able to speak for a quiet kind of humanism that commits them not so much to the presence (or absence) of God as to the presence of man.

Camus and Silone seek to shore up the human enterprise in a time when we feel abandoned by God by restoring sacredness and trust to the relation of man to man. Silone describes the curse of our time as insincerity and lack of faith between man and man. To break down this insincerity we must learn to talk with one another; and we must be willing to endure silences with one another, because there is a kind of silence which opens us to one another.

Camus accepts the cosmic homelessness that Franz Kafka makes so real to us. He suggests that man is up against a mute and abandoned universe; nothing is at the center and nothing is at the end. We would do well to take his description seriously, for it is an emphatically modern one: he speaks for secular man, for the man of this world, who is all around us. Camus' fundamental assumption is that man faces a situation arising out of a great abdication in the City of God itself.

But far from being paralyzed by it, he is moved to decisive action. He has no one to look to but himself. There is no information agency for the twentieth-century pilgrim: he must find the way for himself. It is up to him to decide where he will go.

The testimony of contemporary writers like Camus and Silone is being heard by theologians and churchmen today. It is an accurate articulation of the experience of men both within and without the churches.

One of the first theologians to sense this dramatic shift in sensibility and to give it theological expression was the German theologian Dietrich Bonhoeffer. Curiously enough, Bonhoeffer's principal impact has been in England and in the United States rather than in Continental Europe; this is so even though his thought is deeply rooted in the German situation of the 1930s and 1940s. His thought is seminal in each of the areas we are considering here.

Dietrich Bonhoeffer was active in the resistance of one segment of the Lutheran Church to Nazism in the 1930s. He was arrested after taking part in an abortive plot on Hitler's life and executed by the Gestapo on April 9, 1945. While in prison he continued to write, and many of his letters and papers were published posthumously as *Letters and Papers from Prison*. This slim volume has had an immeasurable impact on contemporary theology. Although he has been dead for more than twenty years, many of Bonhoeffer's ideas have a freshness and a pertinence that few contemporary theological writings can match.

Bonhoeffer calls our world a world "come of age." He is thinking of a Europe torn by two world wars, two totalitarian systems (communism and fascism), and a major depression. He feels that no generation has as little ground to stand on as ours. It is a world which no longer needs the God-hypothesis, which no longer needs God to account for that which we cannot explain in morals, politics, or science.

Bonhoeffer does not decry this coming of age. For him, it means that the world has taken over much Christian truth (without giving credit where credit is due, for the most part); only those who want to go back to childish dependence on God resent a world that goes about its business without God. Bonhoeffer suggests that the attack of some Christians on the adulthood of the world is pointless, ignoble, and un-Christian. For

Bonhoeffer, history gives eloquent testimony of God's willingness to be edged out of the world. To live in this world means that we are forever standing before the God who makes us live in this world without using him as an answer for questions we cannot answer ourselves.

Bonhoeffer also speaks of "religionless Christianity." For him religion is a place on the borders of life reserved for God. The God of religion is the God of the gaps, the God we insert into our own thinking and acting in order to explain things we do not understand. He is the God we invoke to rescue us from situations we cannot handle by ourselves. Bonhoeffer suggests that "religious" people speak of God when human resources fail, when human understanding reaches an impasse. The decisive difference between Christianity and all other religions is that most religion move man to look to God when in trouble in the world. Man uses God as a God out of the machine (*deus ex machina*). Christianity, on the other hand, "directs him to the powerlessness and suffering of God; only a suffering God can help."

Because the world has come of age, has "grown up," it is no longer dependent on the supportive, problem-solving God. If we have come of age, we must not expect God to treat us like children. We must reject the God of the subway posters who will help us adjust to life, hold our families and friendships together, and help us get along better in the world. Every attempt on man's part to bribe or trick God into entering his religious life is doomed to fail. When men seek to do so they are trying to use God, and God refuses to be used.

The church has always been uncomfortable with men whose self-assurance and independence made belief unnecessary for them. The traditional response to such a man was "You just wait; one of these days you'll be brought up short, and then you'll find out that you need God, just like the rest of us." Bonhoeffer contends that we must learn to live as if God were not there. "The God who is with us is the God who forsakes us." Perhaps a little crow-eating is in order for Christians today. It is too easy to complain about the worldliness of this age. Bonhoeffer urges the

Christian to live in the secular world. To renounce the world, which is doing very well without God, is no way to find God. If he is to be found at all, he is to be found in this world.

Bonhoeffer invites us to accept this world as a world the base of whose culture is no longer sacred, but profane: a world in which it is not God (or the gods) who fills our needs and solves our problems, but man himself. The world itself, man himself as he lives in the world, fills needs and solves problems, not God. The modern history of the church is a chronicle of the erosion of its authority as need-filler and problem-solver. As Bonhoeffer's hearers we echo his plea that God must no longer be asked to do what man can do for himself and for one another: to forgive, to bind up the broken-hearted, to talk with—and listen to—the lonely, to face the fear of death. These are problems of this world that must be met by the world itself.

This means that man doesn't really need God at all. God is not necessary to man, or to the world. The modern world can (indeed, does) get along quite nicely without God. William Hamilton suggests that this affirmation makes volumes of Protestant preaching, evangelism, and Christian education look remarkably thin. The question raised by the contention that man can get along very well without God is: Can we define the Christian as the godless man?

Modern Protestants are divided on this question. Some consider our time as the time of the death of God that Nietzsche's madman announced. Others contend that our view of God needs a radical facelifting but stop short of proclaiming the event of the death of God itself.

Not long ago the English revue *That Was The Week That Was* produced a whimsical lyric (by Sydney Carter) that parodies some of the ideas and concerns of Bishop Robinson:

> Your public image, now, O Lord
> Is really out of date,
> And we'd better get another
> Before it is too late.

Refrain: All Glory Laud and Honor to
          I really don't know who,
          But keep on swinging the censer round
          The way you used to do.

          The old man with the whiskers
          You see upon the wall
          You'd better look the other way
          He isn't there at all.

          Half the things the Bible says
          I don't believe are true
          And maybe I'm a bishop but
          I think the same as you.

          God without religion
          Is what we want today:
          You've got to tell the truth
          Although they take your crook away.*

Concern with "the public image of God" is not restricted to satire. Every claim made for the presence and power of God in this world is being challenged, a challenge coming not from faithless critics and satirists who stand outside the Christian community but from serious, responsible bishops, clergy, theologians, and laymen who call themselves Christians.

These men ask the same questions writers and philosophers have asked for a long time, and many of them boil down to: Does God care about the world? And if so, how does he do it?

The French paleontologist Teilhard de Chardin expresses a radical man-centered view of human affairs when he suggests that "we have become aware that in the great game that is being played we are the players as well as the cards and the stakes." He says this not simply as a scientist, but as a Jesuit priest. He is testifying to the fact that we can no longer claim that God interferes creatively in the game we call "the affairs of men and of nations." We have posed the question "Does God care for men?" This much of an answer can be offered here: He does not care in

* D. Frost and N. Sherrin, eds. *That Was The Week That Was*, London, W. H. Allen, 1963.

a way which leads him to interfere in human affairs. Or perhaps he is unable to do so. What Teilhard and Camus and so many others suggest simply reinforces a truth about God that men have always been slow to accept—that, in human terms, God is powerless and impotent.

The modern novelist speaks of God's absence from the world. Existentialist writers like Jaspers speak of a world from which God has been driven forth. Bonhoeffer tells us that "only a suffering God can help." Each of these conceptions of the Divine is in its way a preparation for one of the most startling theological proclamations of modern times—the echo of Nietzsche's "God is dead."

Thomas J. J. Altizer, one of the theologians the press have lumped together under the title "The Death-of-God theologians," has said that "the task of the theologian is to affirm, and even to will, the death of God." For him, the death of God is an event: "God has died in our time, in our history, in our existence." What does it mean to say that God is dead? Is it any more than a rather startling way of saying that for the most part, God is unreal today? Or is it simply a way of saying that it is meaningless to speak of God in the language of supernatural force and human relationship because such God-language is no longer related to human experience?

William Hamilton insists that it means these things, and more. The dominant theological "line" in the twentieth century has rested on the assumption that, while we cannot know God, he has made himself known to us. The use of analogies from human experience papered over the sizable crack in the wall of this structure. Hamilton suggests that the situation has deteriorated now, and that now God doesn't make himself known to us, even as an enemy. He is not talking about the absence of the experience of God that we find in so much contemporary literature; he is talking about the experience of God's absence.

Two points of marked similarity among the Death-of-God theologians are worth mentioning here. First, their acceptance of a radically profane, secularized world, and second, their willingness to stick to what they themselves know and experience. Paul Van Buren, Assistant Professor of Theology at the Episcopal Theological Seminary of the Southwest in Austin, Texas, speaks of this self-imposed limitation in this way:

In almost every field of human learning, the metaphysical and cosmological aspect has disappeared and the subject matter has been "limited" to the human, the historical, the empirical. Theology cannot escape this tendency if it is to be a serious mode of contemporary thought, and such a "reduction" of content need no more be regretted in theology than in astronomy, chemistry or painting.

This statement echoes the theme of contemporary writers like Camus and Silone, who seek to examine and describe man's situation in terms of the "human, the historical, the empirical" mentioned above. The New Theology is sometimes referred to as evidence that the "secular mind" with which theology must communicate is also at work within the church. Hamilton, Altizer, and Van Buren are the most radical exponents of such theological posture. Although they differ considerably in temperament and in point of view, there are thematic similarities which bind them together.

Altizer is the most flamboyant of these thinkers. He examines the problems posed by the death of God in terms of the sacred and the profane. How, he asks, can man's connection with the sacred be restored? He suggests that we seek the sacred, not by saying "no" to the radical profanity of our age, but by saying "yes" to it. He describes the task of the theologian as the uncovering of religious meaning in a world "bathed in the darkness of God's absence." It is not easy to affirm the death of God, but Altizer refused to draw back from the offense, the "scandal," of such an affirmation. Indeed he suggests that the theologian must accept the tension of saying a "no" that can become a "yes" and a "yes" that can become a "no." To say that God is dead is to be willing to undergo the darkness of the divine absence from the world and to await the possibility of a new showing-forth of the presence and power of God.

Altizer sees Jesus as a Nietzschean figure who was "free of history"; he looks forward to liberation from the absence of the sacred to its opposite through a "dialectical movement" of history. By dialectical movement he means that affirming the full reality of the secular, "worldly" character of modern life will somehow bring the opposite, the sacred, into the world. He envisions man as accepting, even willing, the death of God and participating in the utter desolation of the profane while he awaits the new epiphany of the sacred.

Altizer's acceptance of the world, of what he calls profane, is his "yes"—but it is a hostile "yes." He sometimes speaks as if the world were somehow willfully concealing the sacred from man, and that under persistent attack it will give up its secret.

The second of the Death-of-God theologians is Thomas Van Buren. For Van Buren it is meaningless and irrelevant to speak of God in the language of supernatural force because such God-language is not related to contemporary experience. He contends that there is no trustworthy language about God, a result in part of his commitment to analytical philosophy. He does not speak of the loss of the experience of God. He is talking about words, and about how difficult it is to find words that can be used to speak about God.

His style, then, is to stick as close as possible to what we can experience and know in ordinary ways. Something has happened in his experience which has made it impossible for him to speak about God. In his own precise way, Van Buren too proclaims the death of God. This is not to say that he ceases to talk of Christianity. Just as for Altizer the Christian is the "waiting man," so for Van Buren the Christian without God is drawn to the figure of Jesus as standing before and sharpening awareness of neighbor. He speaks of a contagious quality about Jesus: Jesus gives focus to the Christian life; it is he who calls us into the world to serve him there.

William Hamilton mentions three motifs in the emerging radical theology of today which are important, in varying degrees, to each of these writers.

The first theme has to do with the experience of loss that these theologians call the death of God. The phrase *death of God* raises many more questions than it answers. First of all, it has been used in many different ways over the years. The nineteenth-century philosopher Hegel used it as a symbolic way of expressing the inner meaning of the crucifixion. Friedrich Nietzsche uses it to point to an event that actually occurred in the last century. While Thomas Altizer accepts Nietzsche's interpretation, Hamilton seems to avoid the idea of "event" and speaks of the death of God as a metaphor that describes something happening to a particular group of modern Christians today. He makes clear his preference for this particular metaphor over others—like "absence of God," "withdrawal of God," "eclipse of God," or "the hiddenness of God"—because he believes that something irretrievable is portrayed by the metaphor of death. The other terms still exist quite comfortably within the classical tradition, which speaks of the dialectic between God's presence and his absence, which assures us that the God who is far off will be near, that the God who is hidden will make himself known. These radical theologians insist that this dialectic has collapsed; the phrase *death of God* points to this reality.

The second motif in the Death-of-God theology has to do with the meaning of Jesus for one who accepts the death of God. Hamilton maintains that the time of God's death is also the time of obedience to Jesus. This implies that the Jesus of the New Testament can in fact be known in such a way that discipleship to him—to his life, his words, his suffering, his death—is a center for Christian life in the world. The Christian, then, is the man bound to Jesus, obedient and responsive to him. This Jesus, however, is not the ancient, rarefied Jesus of Nazareth who can be known only if we are closed to the possibility of his contemporary presence. Rather it is the Jesus to whom we repair, the one before whom we stand, the one whose way with others must also be our way because there is something distinctive about his life that we do not find anywhere else.

The Christian Jesus is the Jesus who is fully manifest in a

present moment of time. Altizer considers Nietzsche's *Thus Spake Zarathustra* one of the most profound portraits of the Jesus who is present in our time. In this work, which is intended to be an ironic reversal of the Christian gospel, Zarathustra proclaims that the tyranny of time in a past and external form is the deepest obstacle to freedom and life and joy in this world. He speaks to the madness of the melancholy Nosayer in this way:

All "it was" is a fragment, a riddle, a dreadful accident—until the creative will says to it, "but thus I willed it." Until the creative will says to it, "But thus I will it; thus shall I will it."

Hamilton has been asked why he has chosen Jesus as the object of his obedience. He has no easy answer to this question. What he does say, candidly, is that it is to Jesus that he is drawn. It is to him that he has given his allegiance, and it is a free choice, freely made.

The third motif Hamilton notes is the optimism of radical theology in general, and of the Death-of-God movement in particular. By optimism he means neither inevitable progress nor insensitivity to tragedy and suffering. What he does mean is that radical theology is relating itself to a new feeling of hope and optimism in American life today. Traditional theology has tended to be somewhat hesitant about endorsing the world. The Christian has been led to believe that this world is not his real home and that this life is but a shadow of the rich, full life to come. The new optimism of which Hamilton speaks is trying to discipline itself to saying "yes" to the world of rapid change, automation, new technologies, cybernetics, and the mass media. This new optimism heralds the end of the time of alienation, of hostility and an entrance into a world of technology, speed, and the secular city.

Hamilton finds this optimism in today's Negro revolution; the radical theology seeks to learn from this and other decisive movements in our national life. He sees some evidence to suggest that American theology is living in the present, and that the American theologian is now open to the logician and the philosopher, the psychologist and the psychoanalyst, the literary critic and the social scientist. It is no longer possible for the American theologian to return to the past. There are hopeful signs that he looks forward to the future.

Hamilton, then, sees three themes emerging in the radical theologies of today: the death of God, obedience to Jesus, and a new optimism. This movement involves a small group of theologians, but their influence is already being felt in areas where the church's ministry is in direct contact with the so-called secular world.

The New Theology and the Church

If contentions about the powerlessness, absence, and death of God are taken seriously, what can we say about the nature of the church? Hamilton suggests that the problem is not that he and other radical theologians have no doctrine of the church. Rather it is that, professionally, he must work with three distinct understandings of the church, but only the third makes sense to him.

The first understanding of the church defines it by its four classic marks—unity, holiness, catholicity, and apostolicity. In all ecumenical discussions, and in the growing Roman Catholic–Protestant dialogue, he must see the church in this way in order to carry on conversation. The second way finds the church wherever the word of God is preached and the sacraments are rightly administered. This is a working definition, but falls short because it says little about the world and can result in self-righteous insulation and isolation from "where the action is."

The third definition of the church has become a working definition for the radical theologian. For him, the church is present whenever Christ is being formed among men in the world. Exponents of the New Theology in the Church of England make a significant distinction between the "extrinsic church" and the "instrinsic church." The extrinsic church is that group of people who are willing to proclaim and witness to the fact that God is the "being," the force, the person moving the world in some purposeful direction. The intrinsic church is made up of all those who live in terms of love and concern and responsibility but have not responded to the claim that Jesus is the Christ. Those who are outside the intrinsic church, then, are those whose style of living is nonloving, nonresponsive, and closed to others.

Exponents of the intrinsic church emphasize that formal initiation, regular financial support, and churchgoing are not all there is to being a part of the church. They place great emphasis on quality of life and show less concern for loyalty to the institutional church.

The place and posture of the church in the world needs redefining in every age. As Kierkegaard wrote: "Every generation has to begin all over again with Christ." The church in every age hesitates between two great choices: security, which simply draws on what has gone before and stays on safe ground, or insecurity in the world, which comes with moving out of safety into danger. To put it another way, the church is either a fortress against the world or the servant of the world.

What might be called the fortress-church response to the world is very much with us: it is the tendency to draw into itself in order to recover its uniqueness. Such a view of the function of the church usually involves the exclusion of the forces of change that are shaping the secular world. It places strong emphasis on the institutional church as mediator of truth, regulator of behavior, and dispenser of salvation.

The New Theology contends that the church can no longer afford the luxury of acting like a fortress against the world. Either the church risks death itself by living as servant to the world, or else it withdraws into itself and dies the slow spiritual death which comes of self-centeredness, irrelevance, and despair. Bishop Robinson addresses himself to this challenge; in a recent article in *Look* magazine he is quoted as saying:

The structure of the Church as a religious club will inevitably find itself being squeezed out. If the efforts of the Church are put into keeping it, it will survive as a museum piece, doomed to frustration.

As the walls begin to fall, we'll discover whether this will find us exposed for death or stripped for action. I welcome this. It is in fact a liberation. It will be a great release of power and energy.

The walls of the fortress-church have begun to fall already; many have already gone into action. The civil rights movement has moved many churchmen to risk life and limb in the world. Men are ready with new ideas; they are ready and willing to "get involved." And most important, they are willing to listen to what the world is saying to them. Daniel Berrigan tells us that "the real effort, never really done with, is to discern what Christ is saying to us from within the real world . . . all else is a mortician's job, or a child's game." To put it another way, we need to recognize man's struggle for a human world as the sphere of decisions of faith. The world, after all, goes about its business quite well without the church. Many unbelievers surpass Christians in the purity of their outlook and their awareness of neighbor. They are the intrinsic church because they live lovingly and responsibly in the world.

This is unsettling to a society of believers which assumed that it contained and expressed the true conscience of man, once and for all. In *The New Creation as Metropolis* Gibson Winter develops the idea of "the servant church." He lays it on the line when he writes:

The underlying thesis of these considerations is that the world is radically changed; a wholly new relationship of Church to world is called for in our time. This new relationship can be described as the servanthood of the laity—the servant church.

Winter contends that "the contemporary world has a new universe of meaning, a radically different social structure and problems peculiar to its own time." The church's place in this new, radically different, self-sufficient world is not what it once was. If the church is to become servant to the world it is not present as custodian of the past, but as witness to man's hope for the future.

The servant church talks to the world, and in the world, not about God but about man. Some years ago Karl Barth accused Rudolf Bultmann of substituting anthropology for theology, to which charge Bultmann replied:

I would heartily agree: I *am* trying to substitute anthropology for theology, for I am interpreting theological affirmations as assertions about human life.

This gives us common ground for a dialogue between servant church and world—the struggle for humanity. The servant church makes the values that men cherish for themselves universal; it confronts man with his responsibility, not only to and for himself but also to and for others. The message of the servant church is simply this: that it is man's responsibility to shape his own future, and this fashioning dismisses any ultimate claim for any structure in this world and risks suffering with men in their struggle to become what they were born to be.

How, then, is the church to talk with the world? The New Theology is almost unanimous in contending that it is self-defeating to try to verbalize the Christian faith in traditional language. Indeed, the so-called hard radicals suggest that it is impossible to talk about the faith at all with the world. This is, in part, because the world is too much with us, and we are too much with the world. The distinction between church and world, between Christian and secular man, between sacred and profane, is difficult to make today; this is not a curse, but a blessing. It means that the church cannot be content to talk about the faith or to describe it: it must live it. Christian lives today do not make claims; they show forth what Daniel Berrigan "calls a kind of radiant symbolic activity. There are no proofs, but many signs. In the lives of such men human issues, world issues, are quietly assumed to be Christian issues, and men put their lives on the line."

This style of standing within the world is basic to any and all specific decisions and actions. Ignazio Silone puts it this way:

[It is] not a matter of putting new formulas, new gestures, or shirts of a different color into circulation, but rather a matter of a new way of living. . . . It is a matter of becoming a new man. Perhaps it is sufficient to say that it is a matter of becoming a man, in the real sense of the word.

A new way of living: life that is not overly interested in proving anything about itself, or about the character and quality of its mission in the world; life that is concerned with becoming a man, in the deep sense of the word.

The New Morality

These concerns are articulated in another area of the New Theology called the New Morality. The leading advocates of this contemporary Christian ethical stance are John Robinson and H. A. Williams of England and Joseph Fletcher of the United States. The New Morality is a product of a renewed interest in Christian ethics as a discipline concerned with making decisions, with discovering oneself in the midst of decision-making, with acting like the person the life of Christ makes you. Its emphasis is not law but love, not prescribed actions but persons acting lovingly toward others. It is concerned with persons who face situations in which decisions must be made. It begins with only one ultimate norm for decision, Christian love (*agape*).

The New Morality is not new in any ultimate sense. What makes it new is its freshness and its tentative, searching approach. Bishop Robinson makes no claims for novelty. He speaks of the New Morality as "none other than the old morality, just as the new commandment is the old, yet ever fresh, commandment to love." Joseph Fletcher reminds us that St. Augustine reduces the whole Christian ethic to a single maxim: "Love and *then* what you will, do." He also reminds us that he did not say "Love and do what you please." A contemporary Roman Catholic theologian, Hercule Gilleman, has written an important work, *The Primacy of Love*, in which he underscores the importance of this posture for present-day ethics.

Robinson sees the New Morality as but a part of a revolution that has long since broken out in both theology and ethics. Just as he moves toward reassessing his doctrine of God, so too he seeks to reassess Christian ethics with reference to this revolution. This attitude is shared by Harry Williams and Joseph Fletcher, whose concern is with the person rather than with precisely what the person does, with the actor rather than with the act itself, with motive (or motives) rather than with prescribed behavior, with love rather than with law.

The revolution to which these men are responding affirms the priority of persons. Too often the old morality has appeared to dismiss this priority for the sake of principles and laws. The non-Christian writer of our day is certainly far ahead of the Christian writer when it comes to being aware of human beings and their needs, to feeling compassion for persons in the midst of the world. Peter Berger reminds us that it is one of the ironies of history that Christian ethical thought often finds itself in the antihumanist camp.

The writings of Robinson and H. A. Williams are not systematic; it would therefore be unjust to try to reproduce the structure of their ethic as a logical system. However, Bishop Robinson does write at length on how the New Morality differs from traditional and conventional ethical thinking. Because of his apologetic (explanatory) approach, let us consider his ethic from this point of view.

First, he suggests that an "interpretation" needs to be made between the New Morality and the old, contending that each side must try to understand and respect the other as having an equally genuine concern for the fundamentals of Christian morality. He begins by examining the tension that must always exist between the fixed and the free, the constant and the changing, the absolute and the relative. To him, what the New Morality is saying to us is that we need not fear flux: God is in change as much as in *status quo*, and as Christians we are free to change and grow and not merely to conserve what we already have and are.

Robinson goes on to discuss the tension between law and love. The old morality, he writes, starts from the position that the Old Testament comes before the New. In that sense law has a priority over love. Love builds on law, and comes to fulfill, not to destroy it. The Christian needs the law for himself, he needs it for his children, and he certainly cannot dispense with it for his society.

The New Morality, on the other hand, starts from facts the old morality would not wish to deny but does not emphasize as much as the new. The New Morality insists that the Christian is under grace and not under law. The law is tutor, not master. It insists on the priority of love in every sense except the temporal —for Jesus makes all the law and the prophets hang on this one command. He suggests that love is the end of the law not merely in the sense that it abolishes it as grounds for the Christian's relationship with God or with one another.

It is this emphasis that is so important for the New Morality. Robinson suggests that the Holy Spirit is speaking to us through the deadness of the old morality for so many people; what the spirit is showing us is what we have heard from the beginning: nothing fundamentally new but, when we feel its power, fresh and explosive.

Robinson, then, would claim that the New Morality differs from the old in emphasis. He looks to the Sermon on the Mount for scriptural warrant for the approach implicit in the New Morality. In Jesus' treatment of the fourth commandment (Remember the Sabbath day, to keep it holy) the law is undercut as law altogether when he subjects it to the concern for which it stood. He claims that his actions are the fulfillment rather than the negation of the law. Jesus and the writers of the New Testament carefully avoid the possibility of even *apparently* dividing life up into various "cases" or "instances" which, as such, could be prejudged in a legalistic manner. The New Morality is corporate and social rather than privatistic and individualistic. Robinson points out that most of those who are concerned with the revolution in Christian ethics have come to this position through engagement in problems of social ethics.

There is a comic desk sign that reads DON'T CONFUSE ME WITH FACTS—MY MIND IS MADE UP! Joseph Fletcher reminds us that this is no joke for ethics. It points to the kind of insecurity that makes people long for an ethical system prefabricated for them. It makes them look at ethics as a set of rules to invoke automatically in difficult situations. Ethics that demand decisions made in the midst of a situation are too full of variables for them: they prefer the eternal verities handed down by a higher authority, whether God, Church, State, or University.

As life and society become more and more complicated, our ethical decisions grow increasingly difficult and complex. The security of a prefabricated code means that one must fit life to rules, and this does violence to one's ability to look at the facts of his life and of the lives of others. Legalism—strictness with regard to the law—always emphasizes conformity and order, while "situation" ethics emphasize freedom and responsibility.

The old morality is also contrasted to the New in terms of the difference between the transcendent and the immanent in Christian ethics, between the deductive approach and the inductive. The old morality begins from the deductive, the transcendent, and the authoritative. Its stress is on the revealed character of the Christian moral standard. It starts with Christian principles that are valid "without respect of persons" and then applies them to particular situations and persons. Each case is considered on its own merits.

The New Morality does not deny this dimension of Christian ethics. It merely uses a different approach. It begins with the fact that theology is to be understood as an inductive discipline, proceeding from the particular to the general, starting from persons rather than principles, from experienced relationships rather than revealed commandments. It does not disclaim authority; its authority is of a different kind. Its authority is neither theocratic nor autonomous, but rather what Tillich calls "theonomous." *Theonomy* is the authority of the divine light shining through Jesus' words and works, authenticating him and his mission. It is related to Tillich's effort to push beyond supranaturalism and naturalism to a third position in which the transcendent is nothing external or "out there" but is encountered in, with, and under the *Thou* of all finite relationships as their ultimate depth and ground and meaning.

In ethics this means accepting the actual concrete relationship in all its particularity as the basis of moral judgments. It means, in the depth of that unique relationship, to meet and respond to the claims of the sacred, the holy, and the absolutely unconditional. For the Christian, it means recognizing the unconditional love of Jesus Christ, "the man for others," as the basis of every relationship and every decision.

In *Christian Morals Today* Robinson illustrates the theonomous authority of Christ's *agape* with the foot-washing passage in the fourth gospel. "You call me Master and Lord," he says, "and rightly so, for that is what I am," but the sole authority Jesus would exercise is that of "the man for others." Robinson spells this out in *Honest to God* when he writes:

This is what it means for the Christian to "have the mind of Christ," to let his actions be governed, as Jesus enjoined, simply and solely by the love with which "I have loved you," or, in St. Paul's words, to "let your bearing towards one another arise out of your life in Christ Jesus." Life in Christ Jesus, in the new being, in the Spirit, means having no absolutes but his love, being totally uncommitted in every other respect but totally committed in this.

Love, then, is the only absolute. Only love can search out the deepest need of the other; it alone can afford to be completely open to the person in the situation, meeting the situation on its own merits.

In a splendid essay in *Soundings* entitled "Theology and Self-awareness" H. A. Williams gives us a somewhat startling example of how that love which can search out the deepest need of another sometimes leads to a violation of the "moral law." In the film *Never on Sunday* a prostitute in the Piraeus is picked up by a young sailor. In her room he becomes nervous and afraid; this is not because he thinks he is violating any laws, or rules, but because he mistrusts his capacity for physical union. He is a victim of destructive doubts about himself, not of moral scruples. The prostitute gives herself to him in such a way that he goes away with dignity and self-respect, a deeper, fuller, more complete person than before. Williams submits that this is "an act of charity which proclaims the glory of God." There is healing here, "and where there is healing," writes Williams, "there is Christ, whatever the Church may say about fornication."

We must all have the courage of Jesus and say to ourselves "It is written . . . but I say unto you." This is a great risk, but at the heart of Jesus' teaching and example is the insistence that we must be ready to risk everything if we want to find our lives. Sigmund Freud has shown us that evil consists of refusing to give through that fear which masquerades as morality. Williams suggests that the essence of sin is to organize oneself as if he were justified by his works. In other words, the essence of sin is to hide oneself behind the mask of self-contained obedience to the moral law. This is the importance of St. Paul's discovery that we are not justified by good works, but by faith. And as Kierkegaard argues in *Sickness unto Death*, the opposite of sin is not virtue, but faith. By faith we do not mean assent to a number of doctrinal statements. Nor is faith a conviction, since a conviction is the result of an intellectual processs concerned, for the most part, with amassing evidence. Williams suggests that faith is "confidence in life, the trustful attitude of a child belonging to a loving family. . . . Faith . . . is intuitive. It is a given (not acquired) certainty that the forces on our side are greater than the forces opposed to us."

The New Morality is optimistic about man. It suggests that the man who lives in love lives in Christ; therefore he acts as he sees fit in each particular situation. The law has a legitimate function as a guideline for action, but is never absolute. There is but one absolute, and that is Christian love. The New Theology does not point to a hand-list of prescribed actions; it suggests a style of standing before God and the world: a posture that precedes, and is basic to, every action and decision in the life of man.

The Campus Scene

Robert McAfee Brown describes the so-called new student as a member of "a revolting generation." He belongs to a new breed;

he is in revolt, and to some this is revolting in more ways than one. Just as college students were called "the silent generation" in the fifties and were, for the most part, conventional, cynical, and detached from the political and social movements of their day, so the students of the sixties attract such adjectives as *rebellious, nonconformist, angry, anarchistic,* and *revolutionary.*

Many of the same middle-aged critics who condemned the indifference of the fifties are now puzzled and upset by the "misbehavior" of today's militant student. What do these critics want them to be like? Somewhat radical, perhaps, and concerned, even militant—but not like this! "What do we have on our hands?" they moan. "A revolution!" Much of the time it is a revolt in search of a cause, a protest that cannot be ended by "giving them what they want." They are not protesting because things are bad for them, or for others, but because things are what they *are* for others and for themselves.

This is, above all, an *existentialist* revolt. Students are rebelling because they do not feel at home in the world as it is. They find that everything is laid out for them, if they play the game. For the men, the world of business needs and courts them. For the women, there is always the beach wagon, the vine-covered split-level house, and the four children. If a few simple rules are followed, failure is virtually impossible.

Practically every college student understands what is meant by an "identity crisis." He is preparing to live in a society in which the college degree is the "union card," and the business world is a great anonymous charade. If he is to make good in the business world it will not happen so much because of who he is as because of what he can do and what kind of an impression he makes. If he can function in a way that suits the needs of the firm, he is all right. His own needs, aspirations, hopes, and fears are only important if they interfere with his efficiency and productivity.

In addition to his suspicions about the bigness and anonymity of "big business," many of today's students reject the reverence for the *status quo* they detect in the tone and attitude of men in authority. I use the title "a revolting generation" not critically but admiringly. This generation finds the cautious pleas of their elders for patience and obedience and prudence intolerable; they believe that such pleas express a fear of the future and a complacency about the present that they cannot accept. The powers-that-be are endured but not revered. Their wisdom and therefore their authority is challenged; the focus is on change and freedom rather than on stability and order.

It would be misleading to suggest that the political arena is the only battlefield for the "new student" of today. He is drawn to the political because it displays so many of the symptoms of hypocrisy and decay that he sees in our society. It is also an area in which he can gain recognition and exercise power, although the student protests against the Vietnam war are much less glamorous than the civil rights protests of the earlier sixties. His basic concerns have to do with what we might call his inner life as an individual: Who am I, really? How can I keep from being crushed by the great leveling forces of my world—conformity, the mass media, the computer, organizational bigness? How am I to live? Do I really have sexual freedom? And if I do, how do I use it? Is it all right to experiment with erotic experience? What about drugs? Is it all right to use them? What really counts in my life? And, perhaps most important, How do I communicate with others?

These questions are not new to students. What is significant is that for the most part, today's students take for granted that they must depend on their own resources for answers. This is but one symptom of what existentialist philosophers have called the experience of having been thrown into an alien world, a world in which one does not feel at home, in which one has no roots. We have already spoken of the sense of "loss of presence," which we find in so much contemporary fiction. One of the prices one pays for mobility and affluence today is uprootedness. Fewer and fewer young people are returning "home" to live and to work after their educations. They are on their own much earlier. They feel out of place in a world they did not shape. They see it as a world full of risks and tensions and uncertainties—a world always in danger of blowing up in their faces. It has been said that every generation has a need for roots. This need is intensified in an uncertain world in which uprootedness is the rule, especially for the college student. Every modern society is experiencing the disease of uprootedness today, whether it is Communist or capitalist, developed or developing. The shock of uprootedness in developing countries, in fact, has been even more violent than in our own.

Max Lerner tells a story about the English historian L. B. Namier that sheds light on the need for roots. Namier was a Polish emigré whose family, seeking to be accepted among Polish nobility, had tried to hide their Jewishness from the world—and from their son. After making a new life for himself in England, Namier became a prominent historian of English political life, a staunch conservative, and a dedicated Zionist. Toward the end of his life he was invited to lecture at Hebrew University. He began, in Hebrew, with the great biblical passage of both lament and affirmation: "If I forget thee, O Jerusalem, let my right hand forget its cunning," and he continued to the end of the passage as tears rolled down his face.

What, asks Lerner, is there that the young American feels this way about today? Does he have a Jerusalem? Certainly not America itself, nor its history, since patriotism of such depth would be maudlin. Not Paris as a movable feast, which it was for Hemingway's generation after the First World War. Not organized religion, whose influence and image in the world is too often confused and impotent. Not the university itself, toward which the student feels little affection or loyalty, which becomes an arena for struggle with the enemy—or, at least, becomes the enemy itself. Not one's family and its memories and traditions, because the family is too often the local enforcer of the *status quo* or is simply not there at all. Not even the "New Left," which is a fighting faith for a few but offers little in the way of roots, only a deeper, more intense uprootedness.

How does this generation of students respond to the New Theology? This, of course, is an impossible question to answer, since there is no way of generalizing about the response of great numbers of students who represent different backgrounds, varying political commitments, and the entire spectrum from total indifference to deep commitment to God in Jesus Christ. However, it is quite possible to describe the response of the student who is restless, revolting, and rebellious. He has something in common with the "young Turk" theologians of the church: he has little use for traditional answers and systems and structures. For both student and theologian there is commitment to the institution, whether church or university or country, but this commitment is grounded in a vision of what might be and can be in spite of what they see here and now. As Henry Malcolm points out, many members of the New Left do not want to dissociate themselves from the United States; they protest because they take the stated values and goals and aspirations of their country seriously and find that the actions of their nation often give the lie to what it preaches.

It is also important to note that the New Theology has had considerable coverage in the mass media. It has been described in a range of publications from *The New York Times* to *Playboy* magazine, and this has brought the personalities and ideas of the radical theologians to the attention of many people who would otherwise have moved through life without making any discernible response to ideas about God, Christ, and Church. Many students who are in the process of abandoning the old "church-on-Sunday-golden-rule-*status-quo* Christianity" of their parents have a good understanding of the issues posed by the New Theology. They see it not so much as a challenge to traditional Christianity as a sign that thoughtful, intelligent men in the churches are involved in issues and controversies having little to do with the perpetuation of the church as an institutional power in the world. They also find that churchmen are concerned with many of the issues that animate the student radicals on our campuses today—civil rights, the war in Vietnam, the problems of poverty and the Negro ghetto, and the quality of university education, to name only a few.

It is probably more accurate to say that students respond to the style and spirit of the New Theology than to say that they have made any significant response to its content. Articles in newspapers and magazines have given them a skeletal—and sometimes misleading—introduction to the personalities and issues involved, but such limited exposure has not stirred any significant response among students. We must also remember that in the university, as in society, the proportion of "committed Christians"—individuals who belong to a particular religious denomination and participate regularly in the life of this group—is small. Curiosity about "religious" issues does wax, however, when such issues turn out to be what the world calls political, moral, and social.

Are there similarities between student attitudes toward God-talk, traditional theology, and the church and the maxims of the New Theology already described? First, it must be said that to-day's students are suspicious of and uneasy about talk about God. There is a defiant openness in the attitude of many students today—an openness that precludes acceptance of the proposition that God is working his purposes out in this world. They insist that if one is going to discover what really counts in life, he is going to have to give himself to the enterprise of *man* working out his purposes in the world without reference to God. This defiant attitude has much in common with the response of the Death-of-God theologians who admit the difficulty in believing that God cares for us in such a way that he works his purposes out in this world.

The response of these students to Jesus is also colored by their discontent and restlessness. They find in him a figure who has not sold out to the Establishment; he is a man willing to offend the powers that be in order to protect or help someone in need. They see him as a man willing to live and die for others; Bonhoeffer's description of Jesus as "the man for others" strikes a responsive chord in many young people who have no formal religious ties at all. Jesus' willingness to risk his very life in order to demonstrate that man is more important than any law or custom impresses the student of today. In fact, Jesus' death is much less a scandal and much more a triumph for these students than it is for many churchgoers. This comment to a university chaplain sums up the attitude of many students today: "I don't know whether I'll ever believe in God, but Jesus is my kind of guy."

In spite of this affirmation of Jesus, there is no stampede back to the church. For students the church continues to be a conservative, fortresslike institution which preserves outmoded rituals and speaks a language that means nothing in the outside world. However, the involvement of clergy in political movements and protests has demonstrated to some students that the church is much more than a collection of respectable people who gather together once a week to celebrate something that few of them take very seriously. It is certainly accurate to say that the idea of the intrinsic church proposed by the New Theology comes very close to meeting the needs and expectations of our young people about the church. If the church is present wherever Christ is being formed among men in the world, as William Hamilton has suggested, then many of the "revolting" generation are a part of it, whether they know it or not. If the church is made up of all those who live in terms of love and concern and responsibility, whether they have responded to the claim that Jesus is the Christ or not, many students who have no formal religious commitment are of the church. The New Theology points to a new style of living in and with the world, a style the church exhibits when it unites in the common struggle for humanity. The church as servant confronts man with his responsibility to and for others. This quality of service impresses the student of today.

This is not to say that the extrinsic church—those people who are willing to proclaim that God is the "person," the force who is present in and cares about the world—is of no importance. It is quite significant that attendance at the university chapel at Columbia almost doubled when the Lord's Supper according to *The Apostolic Rite of Hippolytus* was celebrated. This simple service, concelebrated by Episcopalians and Presbyterians, was open to all baptized Christians, who were invited to eat leavened bread and drink wine from a common cup. Services of the word alone seem to lack the sense of solidarity and concern for one another that one sensed in the Hippolytan service. As one student put it: "In the Hippolytan Rite I feel like I'm doing something important with other people. I care about them and I think they care about me."

What this student is saying, I think, is that the worshiper needs to feel that he is participating and that he is doing something with someone else. Services of the word, complete with big-name preachers, do not meet these needs; to be sure, a well-known churchman may draw a large crowd, but a worship experience that permits action together with someone else is just as important. On occasion during the past year I have celebrated communion in The Postcrypt, a coffee house in the basement of the university chapel, and found that the simplicity of the setting and the intimacy of the simple action of blessing, breaking, and eating bread opened up an entirely new dimension of worship for many of the participants. Even though the fifteen or twenty students who took part in a Tuesday afternoon service were invited to sit in the chapel for the service, the emptiness of the building and the formality of the setting was an impediment for some of them. As one girl remarked after one of the services in the Postcrypt, "I like communion much better down here. The place is the right size and I don't feel lost and out of place like I do upstairs."

This student accepts one of the facts of the intrinsic church's life—that it is a missionary community, and that its norms are drawn not so much from history or esthetics as from the need of the world and the presence of Christ in the midst of those who seek to know him.

The church on the university campus is on the frontier. Worshipers are keenly aware of the constant pressure of the secularism of the world in which they live, and yet they welcome concern for and identification with this world. Bishop Robinson has used the phrase *the holy in the common* to express a world-accepting way of looking at the Lord's Supper. He maintains that the Holy Communion is *the* point at which the common becomes the carrier of the unconditional, as Christ makes himself known in the breaking and sharing of bread. For Christianity, then, the holy is the depth of the common; the purpose of worship is not to retire from this world into another world, but to open oneself to meeting Christ in the common and in so doing meet one another.

Students who have participated in simple celebrations of communion in apartments and coffee houses prefer a "common" setting because it underlines Christ's presence there and emphasizes the life they share with one another. The physical nearness of one another makes their witness to their solidarity and to the wholeness of mankind that much more vibrant and joyful. And most important, such a worship experience can focus and deepen our response to those whose lives will never touch ours.

Just as revolution, change, uprootedness, and action characterize both New Theology and New Campus, so too they are becoming the watchwords of campus ministry. The style of ministry on campus has shifted, and continues to shift, from what might be called *ministry to* to *ministry with*. This is much more than a change in preposition; it is a shift that suggests that all the traditional assumptions about the ministry of the church on the university scene be questioned. The first stage in what we might call modern campus ministry is what is commonly called *student work*, in which the church followed its students with a kind of on-campus religious organization or club. For the most part, student work treated the student as someone to be preserved for church membership. The college chaplain, then, became a clergyman on the scene who could help members of his denomination weather the storm of coming of age in the midst of an institution of higher learning.

The results of such an approach are now history. The program of the religious club has often resembled the high school youth fellowship in tone and activity. As a result it attempted to provide a kind of group continuity by using a model commonly found in the parish church. Unfortunately, this led to the creation of a religious enclave or ghetto on campus. In so doing it made it quite difficult for either the student or the minister himself to identify himself with the life of the secular university as it stood. The "godless university" was too often viewed as the enemy, the subverter of the religion of the student who turned to the religious club for protection.

The debt this traditional approach to campus ministry owes to the parish ministry is obvious. Just as the parish minister attempts to organize and "activate" individuals and families who "belong" to him by virtue of their baptism or adherence to his particular denomination, so too the campus minister who operates in terms of the "religious club" tries to gather members of his denomination around him to form a kind of parish-in-miniature. Sometimes this ministry is based on a "pastor-flock" relationship; in a university setting this often becomes a paternalistic charade in which the pastor supplies his sheep with spiritual and moral guidance whether it is asked for or not. At its best such guidance can be invaluable to the floundering adolescent who is trying to get his bearings in an unfamiliar, indifferent, sometimes hostile new world. At its worst it can lead to the reinforcement of childish ideas about the church as a safe refuge from the world and about the Christian life as a spoon-fed existence marked by passivity, dependence, and suspicion toward "the world outside the walls."

Some campus organizations are conscious imitations of the parish and include such parish features as student vestries, women's organizations, and altar guilds. Such an imitation of the parish might prepare the student for participation in the institutional church after graduation from college, but it is extraordinarily parochial and ingrown as it stands on the campus scene. Parochialism—concern for the health and effectiveness of "the parish" itself—leads to a kind of separatism and ingrownness that has no place on the university campus of today.

The second stage in the development of campus ministry might be entitled "The Ministry Discovers the University." Advocates of the religious club sustained an unspoken yet vital suspicion of the university as a heartless, godless institution that exerted a tremendous influence and control over the minds and hearts of the faithful. As the campus minister has become freer and less concerned with keeping the religious club moving, he has discovered that the university is run by persons who share some of the concerns and the same pressures as the students he already knows. He becomes interested in "the ministry to higher education." He describes his ministry as directed to the university as a whole rather than to students alone.

This movement away from the religious club is an important development in active ministries in many universities because it broadens both the concern and the outlook of these operations. It has opened the way to a ministry *with* as well as a ministry *to*. The church itself has become interested in higher education. To be sure, concern with what "the church is doing in the university" continues, but there is considerably more interest among churchmen today in "how the church is serving the university."

Evidence of the trend toward this kind of ministry can be found in two related but distinct areas of activity. First, we find considerable involvement in on-campus organizations and movements that have appeared in response to issues and dilemmas like civil rights, war, and the draft. Second, we discover increasing interest in, and focus on, the challenges the university itself encounters. Campus ministers are in the vanguard of those who are raising questions like "What role should universities play in shaping the future of American society?" and "To what extent does Defense Department sponsorship of scientific research limit the autonomy of the university?" The significance of campus ministry involvement here is that it is often the catalytic force that gives these issues focus and elicits significant action from students and faculty who share these concerns.

This second stage in campus ministry is university-oriented, issue-centered, and focused on "world" rather than "church." It is a significant movement away from the religious-club style and has broadened and deepened its involvement in and commitment to higher education itself.

A third phase in campus ministry emerging today is a variation on what we have called the university-oriented ministry. We distinguish it from the second because of its style rather than its content: a style that has a great resemblance to styles of moving and acting and living described in the New Theology. In fact, we could say that the New Theology opens the way for action in and with the university on a level not possible before. Campus ministers are discovering that they are making contact with members of a university community, not so much in the intellectual realm as in the no-man's land where the individual meets and responds to the issues and challenges of the world. This is cause for celebration, since it means that one is able to meet and talk with persons not as "parson to person" but as "person to person." The campus minister is in relationship, not because someone "belongs" to him by virtue of some ecclesiastical connection but rather because he and someone else are committed to a common task, a common cause, a common challenge to be met.

Such a style means that the "religious professional" must often move and learn in areas in which he has no special proficiency. However, this does not mean that there is nothing distinctive about his function, for he brings a particular frame of reference —the Christian frame of reference—with him. No matter how "incognito" he feels, he still represents a particular religious office or team of campus ministers and a particular faith community. This is, after all, a source of much leverage on our campuses today. A public statement from a chaplain on a controversial issue on campus is always news. Involvement in university affairs seldom escapes notice and response. This is especially true when he takes a position on an issue which is not "religious"—which has to do with the political, social, or economic sphere. This opens the way for talk and action with the so-called uncommitted student, teacher, and administration. It is a mandate to transform one's style of speaking and acting, a transformation that translates words about dedication to this world into action. For many, the consequences of such a radical commitment to the world are too great.

They are afraid that a turning toward the world means a turning away from the church. It means that the church is not the exclusive, or even the dominant, object of one's attention and fealty. They insist that the very life of the church is being challenged, and that certain radical clergymen are following the fickle winds of fad and fashion.

While this may be true at times, it begs the crucial question: what does it mean to minister to, in, and with the university today? The New Theology gives us a valuable lead as we grapple with this question. It suggests that ministry in this world often means moving outward, into indifferent or hostile territory, among indifferent and hostile people. It means that one acts and moves "incognito:" that there is nothing explicit in our style that sets us apart from others. It means that we act without a "hidden agenda," that we do not seek, under cover of secular involvement, to make Christians out of non-Christians, out of the worldly.

This does not mean that our style of ministry is a repudiation of discipleship to Christ. Far from it. It simply means that we do well to talk less and listen better to what the world is saying to us. In this tangled world actions have become much more eloquent than mellifluous phrases, and just being there continues to mean so much more than saying the right thing.

A concrete example of this kind of "practical presence" is the founding and sponsorship of the Postcrypt, mentioned earlier, a coffee house opened by the Columbia Protestant Office in 1965 in the basement of the university chapel. This was one of the first coffee houses begun by a campus ministry in the United States. The campus-ministry staff has always emphasized that this is not a Christian coffee house—its purpose is not to proselytize, to make Christians out of non-Christians—but to meet a need for contact and communication with students that an office with a shingle labeled *Protestant* simply does not provide. Of course, the coffee house would be self-defeating if it did not meet a real need for the university community as well. The coffee house phenomenon in our culture as a whole has become a focus for folk songs, poetry reading, and drama. In a university the coffee house and its focus have a particular significance, since the aspirations and protests of the student generation are reflected in the folk song and the rock' n' roll of today. The Postcrypt has given the staff of the Columbia Protestant Office a splendid opportunity to meet and talk with students in a nonreligious setting. It has given us a chance to mix with students without reference to their denominational or creedal affiliations and commitments. In many instances it has opened the way to significant counseling relationships.

It is possible to look at the activities of the Postcrypt as a kind of secular liturgy. If we define liturgy as "the work of the people" and as a vehicle for the expression of their deepest ideals, concerns, and beliefs, then the gathering of students around a folk singer who both entertains them and leads their singing is a liturgy. The lyrics of folk songs are an important source of knowledge about the concerns of a particular "folk." As Andrew Fletcher wrote in 1703 in "An Account of a Conversation concerning a Right to Regulation of Government": "I knew a very wise man that believed that if a man were permitted to make all the ballads, he need not care who should make the laws of a nation." If we accept Fletcher's premise, then we may assume that the desire of this generation for social justice and political integrity bodes well for the future.

It is both ironic and peculiarly fitting that such a secular liturgy take place under the portico of the university chapel: ironic in that the celebrations in the Postcrypt often appear to be more vital and vigorous than the liturgy performed in the chapel itself, fitting because such gatherings are what the church is all about and are happening within the physical confines of the chapel. The existence of places like the Postcrypt suggests that the intrinsic church might indeed revitalize the extrinsic church.

The Postcrypt has also played a large part in transforming the involvement of the Protestant office in student life itself. First, it is a quiet, intimate place where students can meet, talk, and perform; as such it supplements the rather meager possibilities for such activities on the campus. Second, it has led to the founding of *Sundial*, a burgeoning literary review. *Sundial* began publication in the spring of 1966 and features material from students, faculty, and alumni of Columbia University. This kind of involvement in university-wide activities would have been quite impossible before the establishment of the Postcrypt. In a sense, then, the Postcrypt marked the beginning of an ever-widening circle of involvement in the life of the university.

What styles of ministry will emerge on the campus scene in the next few years can only be imagined. What is clear is that there is no going back to the comfortable sectarian enclave of the past. The New Theology, the New Morality, and the Death-of-God movement point to dramatic shifts in theological and ethical thinking. The campus ministry reflects the same kind of willingness to move out from the secure patterns of the past toward horizons yet unknown.

The Student Radicals
and the Campus Ministry

HENRY W. MALCOLM

1. From the Beaches to the Streets

The contrast often made between the student generation of today and that of the fifties is, in many respects, one of the best barometers of the changing times in which we live. It seems that it was hardly a decade ago that most students were recognized primarily for their "panty raids" and their beach parties. Those were the days when "playing it safe" had become the motto of the vast majority of college-age young adults. It was the quiet generation of the 1950s that heard a long list of deans and commencement speakers calling for them to become involved in the great issues of the day. Today one finds such addresses often so heavily qualified with notes of caution and warning that one wonders, as one campus minister at New York University worded it, "Are these the same commencement speakers who were calling for social action and involvement only ten years ago?" *

Whereas the previous generation of students found it important to spend their time questioning everything from sex to religion, large numbers of young people today on our nation's campuses want to do much more than merely question. They want to act. How they act and what they act upon may be open for debate, but the fact that they insist upon having a place in the events that characterize the "explosive sixties" cannot be seriously doubted.

Perhaps this new activism has something to do with the image of the young President who was, in effect, killed before their very eyes. Many of them recall those days following November 22, 1963, sitting before the television and finding themselves crying. As one coed recalled, "It seemed to me that I was experienc-

* James Harrison, Presbyterian University Pastor, N.Y.U. (In an address to a conference of Metropolitan New York Methodist Ministers.)

ing something deeply pathetic and prophetic about the country in which I lived. All of a sudden I knew why Negroes were being killed in the South. I discovered something which has been buried deep within the American soul, something I call 'the frightening depths of raw violence.' " That young girl discovered the real depth of her own insight when she went to work in Alabama. She found out what nonviolent protest could do to a few white policemen with horses and dogs. She saw how an act of non-violent courage could elicit the hatred and fury of men under moral judgment. She saw with her own eyes a side of her country she had been taught to believe didn't really exist. And she needed no dean or academic to tell her that there is a challenge that now faces her. She learned it in a way that would not let her easily escape wanting to do something about it.

Some have said that the fall of 1960 marked the beginning of the change from the mild fifties to the active sixties. A small band of Negro students held a sit-in at a North Carolina lunch counter and the emotional climate both on and off campus hasn't been the same since. Up to that point it seemed that the civil rights movement was all but completely limited to the actions of older Negroes using boycotts and demonstrations to obtain equal rights for Negroes. The organization known as CORE (Congress of Racial Equality), which had its origins in Chicago under the leadership of James Farmer, hadn't become recognized nationally as a student-oriented group until after the sixties had begun. And yet many of the younger leaders of the civil rights movement, like James Farmer himself, worked as students making their plans and organizing for the future. It took an organization like SNCC (Student Non-Violent Co-ordinating Committee) to express the degree to which students and young people really were beginning to be involved in the movement. (Today, there is little difference between SNCC and CORE.)

Until this time the liberals in power in Washington seemed to welcome the vast influx of youngsters into positions of social commitment. It all seemed to be so much in keeping with the JFK image. Perhaps this is why the Peace Corps had such a meaningful part to play in the plans of the liberals who wanted to use all that youthful energy for constructive political ends. By 1962 there were students in the South, indeed students around the world, selling the success story of the New Frontier. Many liberals felt that social change was the wave of the future, and the youngsters were gladly playing their parts. But what many didn't seem to realize was that such an experience as working in Mississippi or Alabama might not really serve the purpose of those in power back in Washington. As a matter of fact, it might be that the liberal hopes for social change would have to be seriously examined when these young students began to find out just how this society really works. What would it mean to them that such a place as the Deep South exists in a nation like ours? How was it tolerated for so long? What ties did the self-righteous North with its vast industries have with those who wielded power in the "white man's Southland"? What about the other forms of discrimination that were not being seriously challenged in the ghettos and suburbs of the rest of the nation? Did this not really say something about the whole American system? In fact, the liberals who had hoped so eagerly that the idealism of youth would be directed only at those areas where they thought change "should" take place soon found out that the student participation in social change could not be channeled and controlled. Even liberalism itself was to come under the most severe scrutiny; when that happened, the movement that had appeared to be the greatest weapon liberals could have used became known to the nation as "the student radical movement."

The young liberal students began to discover that even "liberalism" was not the real solution to our nation's problems. It certainly was better than the reactionary attitudes of most conservatives, but liberalism was beginning to prove that it really didn't have the radical perception about change that so many young students soon felt was absolutely necessary.

As this sense of a need for change began to spread throughout our nation's campuses, local chapters of CORE and SNCC began to spring up everywhere. The civil rights struggle had become the focal point of attention for that radical change. Older leaders in the movement seemed to feel that Washington had to be dealt with in terms which liberals could understand. For example, liberals seemed to react favorably to numbers and non-violent demonstrations. And so these older leaders staged the greatest demonstration Washington had seen for many years. The March on Washington in 1963 seemed to be the very thing the liberals needed, and responding with their best techniques, they passed a bill.

All of a sudden, the mass media themselves seemed to react and consequently since then have placed a very high priority on reporting the events that have become characteristic of the civil rights movement. But people were still being killed in the South. Negroes in the North were still fighting rats and the winter cold. The students simply observed the facts of life. The legislation was good, but it wasn't enough. The economic and social causes behind modern man's inhumanity to man remained untouched. The plight of the Negro and other minorities continued to deteriorate. All of the statistics remained the same.

It became increasingly apparent to the students who were becoming involved that although the liberals wanted change, they wanted it to take place within a structure that left the individual Negro all but completely at the mercy of political Washington. This kind of change, however, was absolutely contrary to the experience of students working with projects throughout the country. They had learned that a man gets something by action, not by dependence on the good favor of those with political power. Many of the civil rights workers believed, confidently, that it was not the liberals in power who got them favorable legislation. They had obtained it for themselves. The liberal congressmen in Washington were doing nothing more than what was rightfully expected of them. It was television and the press that tended to place the praise upon the congressmen. Somehow, the students and the workers on the scene appeared to be dubious characters in a process that could only be effected from the top (meaning Washington) on down. The students knew that such was not the case.

By 1963 many campuses throughout the nation had civil rights organizations that were trying to engage more student support for action in the movement. Three different areas were known for their activities in civil rights work: the University System of California, the large Midwestern universities, and New York City (with its many campuses). A variety of other colleges throughout the country, some of them in the South and others that were just beginning to create interest, often received information and support from the other more prominent areas. But by the end of 1963 the movement had spread throughout the entire country. Every major campus and a host of smaller ones had students who were involved in the civil rights struggle. The die had finally been cast.

At first, most of the work that had to be done was organizational. This did not seem to pose any serious problems for the campuses involved. But it did introduce the kind of atmosphere that had not been seen since the thirties, when socialist and Communist causes were being advanced. Many old liberals on campus began to draw the analogy and some began to see visions of riots and purges similar to those of the McCarthy era.

But many administrators seemed to feel, at first, that this kind of activity was "good for the students." Some even instituted programs whereby students could participate in certain areas of civil rights work, doing those things that reflected their "natural" capacities as students, such as tutoring and counseling. But even this insight did not fully take into account the realities the students themselves were witnessing. They were not involved because someone needed students to act like students. They were there because the civil rights movement needed people to do anything and everything to change the whole society. Something quite profound had happened to these youngsters. They had begun to learn things not taught in their history books. They had uncovered information the curriculum of the university was not geared to cope with. They began to see just how decisions were made in this society, how interest groups (some of them represented by the various trustees of their universities) tended to reinforce the patterns of social structure that permitted and even encouraged discrimination and segregation. The students learned how universities fit into the socio-political complex, thus operating to feed into this system and serve its ends.

It was not that one could no longer receive an education unaffected by these forces, but one had to reconcile himself to the fact that he was a participant in the system as long as he remained within its structure. The fact that he was involved in what has been called "a knowledge factory," which educated one for ends beyond oneself, was something the student had to face up to. He could attempt to thwart these ends. He didn't have to be educated to fit in, but it was going to be difficult to get what he himself wanted.

Consequently, many began to choose majors in English, philosophy, political science, religion, anthropology, and sociology. These were the areas in which one might have a chance to deal with "issues." But even here there was no certainty that such would be the case. Many professors had become involved with their own professional problems; they found it increasingly difficult to talk about what was going on in society at the present time. And in many cases it was too easy to get a graduate student to teach those courses the professor didn't have time to teach, but even the graduate students themselves had academic pressures to respond to. And so the structure that had already been prearranged by the curriculum continued to function, in spite of these serious limitations. For the student radical, therefore, education itself had become something directly related to the issues of the society. It was itself one of the major issues that had to be confronted and changed. And finally that confrontation took on a visible form in September 1964 at Berkeley, California.

2. *Liberalism Wasn't Enough*

At first the issues seemed to hinge on the right of student organizations to use university space for the purpose of raising funds and soliciting support for civil rights projects. The Berkeley administration believed that it could stand on this point because there was an encroachment on academic life. But the students felt that if large business corporations and industries could have access to the resources of the university, so could the groups fighting for civil rights. They felt that the university had already opened its doors to the outside world, and students themselves had as much right as any other group to introduce the interests of "outsiders" for a possible hearing on campus. As the university took a stand on the issue, the students created, almost overnight, a united front of some twenty campus organizations that rose in opposition to the administration. Out of this action developed something called the "Free Speech Movement," which created a document entitled "We Want a University." Essentially what these students were pointing to was the manner in which that particular educational institution had seriously limited the possibility for an education that could enable one to live meaningfully in our society. They had begun to attack the system. And the events that developed out of that situation have brought to the nation's attention the presence of what had now become known as "student radicalism."

Berkeley was not the beginning of the student radical movement. It was only the most vivid demonstration of a strong undercurrent of resentment and protest against the forces within our society which were increasingly manipulating the lives of everyone. The issues of peace, the bomb, race, poverty, education, morality, and politics had become the crisis problems around which varying ideological positions were developing. And Berkeley provided a perfect example of what was happening on many of the larger campuses throughout the nation. The old assumptions regarding the unqualified "goodness" of education were being called into question. The liberal faith in education was being threatened, not by academics and professional scholars but by a sizable number of students. T. Walter Herbert, Jr., a campus minister at Berkeley, has said:

The liberal faith in education as the main redeemer of mankind is not shared in this radicalism. The way in which universities reinforce evil patterns in the society is very clearly perceived. This scepticism about the power of education to eradicate the ills of mankind makes the radical an apostate from the widely popular cult in American life. The fact that this group was willing to carry on a battle [at Berkeley] which seriously endangered a liberal educational institution testifies to this scepticism. The battle itself has produced a deep sense of shock among those who embrace the liberal faith.*

Actually, the leadership in the Berkeley demonstration was limited to a relatively small group, as is often the case on other campuses. But it is misleading to assume that these few represent the real focus of student radicalism. Several university administrators throughout the country have made a point of this fact and have felt that radicalism was a movement that appealed only to a very small minority of discontented students. But the concerns of student radicals go far beyond the membership statistics of radical student organizations. This is why it is completely wrong to look only to the obvious examples of radicalism on campus to understand the radical movement. There are large numbers of students who share the point of view the radicals dare to make public. This is why any attempt to explain away the movement will always suffer from serious oversimplification.

The same thing needs to be said regarding the image student radicals present to the public. The American middle class often tends to think of such groups and organizations in terms of labels and images. Thus when a news article appears on the radical movement one looks for distinguishing signs to identify the phenomenon. It is seldom recognized by the average reader that these young people come from the same kinds of home and surroundings he does. Their educational background is usually public-school and their interests are not drastically different from those of other young people around the world. The major exception comes when one is faced with the frightening issues that mark our time in history. At this point the radicals take on a different appearance for the public.

* "Reflections on Radicalism," from *Issue: Those Who Make the Waves,* Berkeley, California: Publications Commission of the University Church Council, 1965.

Looking behind all of the epithets hurled at this generation of radicals, one is surprised at the serious lack of understanding by the general public in these vague generalizations. For example, one often hears the label *beatnik* or *hipster* used to describe the students in the movement. Somehow the beards and the sandals on the young men and the long hair on the girls become symbols to the middle class that these are strange and "beat" individuals. Perhaps this is an understandable mistake for many citizens, since the creators of public imagery—the members of the advertising industry—tend to capitalize on the significance of style and fashion, thus "educating" the public to believe that these externals really do have some meaning.

It is true that the "beatnik" experience of a decade ago was the type of phenomenon which reflected something of the feeling among certain intellectuals that participation in modern society was too dehumanizing to tolerate. The "beat" individual who believed that survival could only be obtained by withdrawal from society was characteristic of the fifties. But today it is inaccurate to describe students caught up in the civil rights and radical revolution as beat. The intellectuals who withdrew into their coffee houses in Greenwich Village, San Francisco, and Chicago to read and write their poetry and prose had a different experience from that of the young radicals today. The beats were tired of a society of performance and conformity. They felt a revulsion at the manner in which so many middle-class Americans had become what Paul Goodman has called "an elite that imposed on itself a morale fit for slaves." The student radicals of today have come from the same middle class, but they have discovered that withdrawal will not really help them achieve what they seek. The freedom they are looking for is only partially represented by the manner in which they dress. They refuse to accept the feeling of despair and defeat which marked the "beat generation." Instead there has developed a strange, almost Calvinistic strength, which demands moral judgment upon the forces that are increasingly controlling and "managing" our society. The enemy has become the "brother" who is caught in a downward spiral of impotent masochism. There is nothing beat in the kind of language that demands "freedom now." There is nothing tired about those who are absolutely convinced that the world can be changed and humanized. It is the ones who do not believe this simple truth who are now tired and impotent. It is the liberals who claim that we need time. The liberals are the ones who say, "Well, we shouldn't have gotten involved in Vietnam. But since we are there we are helpless to do anything about getting out. We will just have to make the best of it." This is what it feels like to be "beat." The beards and long hair should not mislead anyone— they are not symbols of rebellion for the sake of rebellion. They are a message to the millions who would like to feel the "cleanliness of dirtiness," the signs of what Freud called "ego gratification." They are doing what feels good instead of what looks good. They realize that much of what they represent is a psychological threat to the "clean" citizens they offend. They are a symbol of something that the "clean" ones fundamentally seek within their own lives.

Another example of the confusion over labels and images can be found in the misuse of the word *cool*. As Marshall McLuhan so perceptively points out, the word *cool* does not have the same meaning for youngsters today that it did for past generations. Young people have learned something of the meaning of "total involvement." But instead of this being defined by conventional patterns of commitment to existing social institutions, it has become something far more subtle. It is involvement through immediate presence and awareness. In other words, it is involvement such as the television set creates and demands.

Things or events are "cool" when one gets "turned on" (like the TV set.) This is why a song by Bob Dylan or a session on "pot" is "cool." They involve the individual totally, not only personally and privately, but also corporately and socially. And those adults who see all this as detachment and withdrawal do not appreciate what total involvement really is. Consequently many adults tend to project their own assumptions upon these young radicals and thus misunderstand what really motivates them.

If we cannot use these old images and labels to identify the radical student movement, how are we to understand it? How can one describe this movement that reflects not merely one segment of our national life, but the depths of modern man's disgust with his world? In one sense we cannot; it is impossible. This is especially true if we were to attempt some kind of a sociological evaluation of their presence in our midst. One cannot describe a few hundred thousand young people, their traits, their dress, and their habits and have presented accurately what they really mean to us. Figuratively speaking, they stand for all who are confronted with adult life and hesitate to enter because they do not see very much that appears meaningful or fulfilling. As Dr. Benjamin Spock has described the life of many young people today:

American children, recent studies show, are being made increasingly anxious by the cold war. Between 25 and 50 percent of our children in U.S. schools today expect nuclear attack. The young ones worry most about being poisoned by fall-out, and being separated from their parents in a disaster, about the maiming or death of their families and themselves. Adolescents speak with some bitterness about the uncertainty of their future, about the possibility of their giving birth to deformed children, about the futility of working hard at school.

Obviously, one ought not to find it surprising that these young people try to make themselves heard. But what the public hears and what it assumes that these young people want to say is often not comprehensible to it. It often appears that the young radicals comprise a united front, but one can soon discover that this is not an accurate picture. It must be remembered that we are not dealing with a massive organization of young people systematically intent on overthrowing the adult world, which has often been the mistaken fear of older individuals who believe that adolescence is always a time of explosive and dangerously violent emotions. Actually this is only true of those who have not examined their own frustrated inner lives. The radicals tend to be much more discerning about matters like these.

Of course there is a high degree of confusion and anger among our younger generation. They are asked to grow up in a world full of deceit and aggression. They are learning that the world is not trustworthy. But it is not at all self-evident that there will be a world worth living in when these youngsters prepare to assume their increasingly predetermined adult roles, and many of them know this quite well.

Thus it is practically impossible to understand what the next generation of citizens is trying to say without sharing something of its perspective. Most of them try very hard to believe that someone really is in control of things, that there really will be a future for them. A great many of these youngsters are forced to repress their fear that the opposite may be the truth, and those who attempt to follow this path become trapped in the peculiar position of doing something that is, for adolescents, quite contradictory. They find themselves "closing off channels for expression of the ordinary normal questioning of adult standards that has been a part of adolescence" for centuries. But those who refuse to accept this manner of fearful trust and dubious conformity now see themselves treated not as adolescents who want the freedom to rebel but as individuals who are suspect and dangerous. They discover themselves cast into the role of antagonists to the structures of social order and security. Thus when one attempts to address oneself to the subject of student radicalism, it becomes absolutely necessary to see the conditions that have come to prevail in our society, conditions that affect all students and young people. The fact that many have chosen the path of challenging the society to change itself ought to help us realize that radicalism is something more than chaos and anarchy. In many respects it is an excellent example of what we mean by the word *responsible*.

3. What is Real in a Society with Artificial Values?

If the radicals want to change things, what changes do they want? What are some of their ideas and how do these relate to the kinds of change they seek? Apparently many seem to think that this generation of student radicals is nothing more than another example of adolescent rebellion. But anyone who thinks this obviously doesn't know them very well. First of all, it is practically impossible to say any one thing about these young radicals that cannot be contradicted in several ways. As a matter of fact, this lack of common imagery is a basic characteristic of the entire movement, which many radicals insist is the true mark of the democratic spirit.

Certainly, a sociologist who makes a study of the movement would be hard pressed to find any empirical method that could provide any meaningful explanation of student radicalism. Second, it is a fact of life within the movement that students never remain in any one group or organization long enough to be completely identified with it. It is practically impossible to label any one of them accurately. As one student put it, "When I was in high school, I got mixed up with a crowd of 'Trotskyites,' but when I came to college I joined CORE and now I am involved with the Independent Committee [on Vietnam]. My ideology has changed several times but my radicalism remains the same. I guess it is because the world remains just as screwed up." As one college coed worded it, "The radical movement cannot be defined at all. That is, it cannot be defined apart from 'issues.' It is the 'issues' which make the movement what it is. And it is the refusal of the government to face up to the issues, to remain stubborn in the face of meaningful human needs, which makes the movement seem radical." Not that all of the students in the movement are themselves self-conscious radicals, nor is it true that all radicals belong to any visible form of the movement, but anyone who seeks to deal with the issues of war and peace, of poverty and abundance, of education and "managed knowledge" is bound to appear radical and threatening to those who think we are doing all that is possible at the present time.

Obviously this concern for issues tends to identify the movement with those issues—they are pacifists because many of them are against all war, or they are "anarchists" because they demand change in such a fashion that they seem to be asking for the impossible. Even the political image "New Left" has some significance relating to certain aspects of the movement. But that label does not accurately describe the ideas of a vast majority of the young radicals. In fact, none of these names really gets at the complex nature of the movement. One must understand that this is a movement responding to the changing world with all its challenges and threats and that old titles and images really can never describe it. What the members of the movement are asking is something fundamentally new in our society, something so new and radical that all of the old political and economic models are no longer viable instruments for comprehending the "new world." And yet, though it may sound contradictory, they find much of what they are looking for buried deep within the past. To explain this seeming contradiction one must realize that they are returning to some of the ideas of the nineteenth century that were never completely adopted, as a consequence of the "artificial nature of the industrial age" and its impact upon Western civilization.

For example, the criticisms Karl Marx leveled at Western capitalistic societies have been betrayed by Communists and capitalists alike. Instead of seeing the age of industrialism as simply another stage in the development of mankind, both political-economic points of view adopted a stance that accepted the industrial world-view as final. This meant that those fundamental human needs that can never be fulfilled with industrial values have been subjected to an ethic and value system that refuses to take those needs seriously. The most obvious danger, however, which the radicals correctly see, is the almost inevitable continuation of industrial values and structures into the age of technology. To them this means the control of abundance for political ends. And control of abundance can only lead to tyranny and the ultimate immorality of man's absolute control of his fellow man.

In attempting to correct the ideological errors of industrialism without ignoring the fundamental changes that had to take place for the modern world to become a reality, the student radicals have often tended to return to three of the most influential minds that helped modern man make the transition from the world of the nineteenth century to the rapidly changing and pluralistic world of the twentieth century: Karl Marx, G. W. F. Hegel, and Sigmund Freud.

The first of these three great thinkers, and perhaps the most influential, was Hegel. Not only did Hegelian thought provide a base for Marx's view of history, it also became the groundwork for much of what is called "contemporary philosophy." Hegel also stands like a great doorway between the world of absolute values and present-day relativistic values. In many ways Hegel was the last great Christian philosopher, the last real idealist. After Hegel, the world found itself in mortal conflict between those who felt that they held a universal view of history (Great Britain, Germany, and Japan; now Russia, China, and America) and those who were striving to find their own place within modern history. Today, we have the ideological struggle between those who believe that a "balance of power" must be maintained in the face of the rising expectations of the "third world" and the "third world" itself. In other words, the Hegelian universalism that attempted to describe the natural development of civilization into a rational community for all men has been replaced by industrial value systems seeking to determine what that history should look like. According to the dialectic of history in which the thesis of capitalism is challenged by the antithesis of socialism, many Marxist radicals find themselves believing that the outcome must inevitably lead to some synthesis of radical change wherein both systems are corrected. Apparently many liberals in our government also feel that this phenomenon is true. In fact, they often speak of the ways in which both Russia and the United States are beginning to look alike in their method of social and economic practice.

But this is where the "democratic radicals" insist that both the Marxists and the liberals have misunderstood Hegel and Marx. They take the impact of technology far more seriously than do those who still think of society in terms of industrial politics. The revolution they point to goes far beyond the aims of socialism or bureaucratic democracy. The working-class man is no longer the model of social revolution, as was the case in the 1920s and 1930s. Instead, today it is the poor, the segregated, the students, and all those who do not have any free participation in determining their own personal future.

In the university, many of these new radicals refuse to adopt the models of either the right or the left in delineating the necessary changes they demand. They point to the technological changes that are about to revolutionize education and society as a whole, and they ask that these innovations be adopted in the place of the older "managed" practices of "education for the national interest." They are fully aware that this older pattern of education means that education serves the ends of those who have the power to manipulate education for their own purposes. This can be either socialistic or capitalistic. To these newer radicals, both systems are immoral. Instead they want information to be free and teachers to be available only to those individuals who want to learn, not those who want to stay in school because they need a particular job or because they want to avoid the draft.

When these radicals confront their universities with these matters of external control, they often receive the response that this is the way things have to be in our society. In returning to Hegel, the student radicals are saying that Hegel's view of one world, one history, is becoming a greater reality than that of the history of the Great Powers. For history to continue to be managed by a few men is to say that history must soon face the fact that freedom and management cannot go together. As Herbert Marcuse has said in his book *Reason and Revolution*, quoting from Hegel, "Man's very nature lies in his universality. His intellectual and physical faculties can be fulfilled only if all men exist as men, in the developed wealth of their human resources. Man is free only if all men are free [a phrase Martin Luther King likes to quote] and exist as 'universal beings.' When this condition is attained, life will be shaped by the potentialities of all the individuals who comprise it. The emphasis on this universality brings nature as well into the self-development of mankind. Man is free if 'nature is his work and his reality.' " *

Thus the student radicals who seem informed about the changing world around them ask why this value of "universality" cannot be fully appreciated. The answer they often receive from their universities is that this is simply another value that must be managed and controlled along with the rest. Thus the conflict becomes one between those who seek two diametrically opposed views of human community. Those who have the task of management insist that society be governed by those who believe in plural truth and who themselves seek to keep the varying truths in educational competition. One must not gain dominance over the rest. But the radicals insist that the control of truth means the same thing as the control of men; that the managers are not really being honest with themselves, because it is quite apparent that competition in educational values means that those who have the resources to see to it that their point of view is maintained and strengthened will do so. If that educational point of view also has political overtones then it will surely become the controlling force in the university. The value of universalism is then treated as a nice ideal but a political unreality.

What the radicals have in mind has its roots in the Hegelian principle "Man is free only if all men are free and exist as 'universal beings.' " This is what the Founding Fathers meant when they said "All men are created equal. . . ." But the radicals realize that the universalism implicit in that statement has fallen into ill repute since the impact of industrialism and capitalism tended to replace it with another value, "competition and management."

With the prophetic insights of men like Marshall McLuhan, Buckminster Fuller, Kenneth Boulding, and Robert Theobald the radicals hear about a new possibility for universal man. The fantastic possibilities that computer technology and communications technology portend for man point directly to a concept of universal man. And they also point to a new and more expanded understanding of community. As one seminary student put it in a

* H. Marcuse, *Reason and Revolution*, Boston, Beacon Press, 1960.

paper he wrote, "The intuition of this college generation is correct. Differentiation has been driven to the psychological breaking point, what McLuhan calls a 'break boundary.' The demands of special occupations have so differentiated out personality types, that an implosion must occur. Personal specialization has required such a lop-sidedness of psychic development, that meaning must once again be reinstated." *

Universalism has become something for the radical that it never really could have been to the utopian in past years. It has become the point of view of those who firmly believe, and have a good case on their side, that there will be no future for man at all if he doesn't begin to recognize the realism of "one world" wherein man is about to become enslaved by bureaucratic forces utilizing the methods of technology to maintain the values of a pretechnological world.

This is what makes the Vietnam war so absurd and evil. This is what makes the existence of poverty in a land of plenty so intolerable. And it is what makes modern education in the form of "packaged education" so completely unnecessary. These are factors that simply do not have to exist in our world today. They do exist because modern man seems to believe that he must control everything—including others. And anyone who believes that man must be controlled, and has the tools of modern technology at his side, can choose only one course: use that technology to control, and if that doesn't work, then use it to destroy.

The impact of Freud upon the student radical movement speaks to this dilemma and goes hand in glove with the significance of Hegel and Marx. In Freud the young radicals see a definition of man that seriously challenges the bureaucratic and managed view of man inherent in all industrial world views. They discover that the patterns of social control which exist today grow out of a belief that man cannot be changed. He must be managed in some sort of socio-political structure. But, as Freud pointed out, the model for this was the classic Oedipal

* Terry H. Foreman, "Changing Thought-Modes: The Future in the Context of History." Union Theological Seminary, 1966, n.p.

family structure. Somewhere in future history this structure must be changed, Freud maintained. This is because it does nothing more than repeat the same patterns of immaturity that the Oedipal structure tends to recapitulate in the individual. Society must go beyond this model. And the young radicals are indirectly telling us that they are living examples of this possibility. They point out that modern society is already in the process of going through this change. Increasingly, all of the natural authority patterns of society no longer have "father" as a model for order. Father has been replaced with a manager who wants to pretend to be father. But this is only because the natural authority of father has been lost in our modern world. The only reasonable replacement for this past structure is some kind of participatory democracy. And when one uses this model in government, in education, and throughout the world, one discovers that a kind of humanistic change is not only possible, it will naturally follow.

4. Someone Has to Take the Risks

The question is often asked: "Why do these young radicals so willingly jeopardize their positions in the society, especially since the vast majority would seem to have so much to lose and so little to gain by their political activity?" They risk going to jail. Many of them suffer real alienation from those who hold the educational and professional strings to their future. They constantly seem to be taking stands on issues which are the most difficult to resolve. Why do they take these risks?

First of all, it is not so certain that radicals really do place their future on the line. Actually, there are many in this country who hold positions of great authority and respectability even though their schooldays were spent in socialist and radical activities. Radicalism does not necessarily lead to professional suicide. On the other hand, there does seem to be something of a difference between the causes fought for by radicals even a generation ago and the issues that concern today's radicals. Actually, many of the radicals' demands during the thirties were adopted by the Democratic party, to such an extent that much of the socialist protest has been drained off and has become respectable political ideology. As a matter of fact, the labor unions, which in the past represented the center of strength of the radical cause, have now become supporters of the established political machines. The old lines of political division have become drastically altered.

The causes that student radicals point to today, however, are the kind of issues socialism can no longer solve. And although there is little agreement on this point among student leftists, there does seem to be an attempt to go beyond the political solutions posed by the radicals of the twenties and thirties. Many young radicals still think of socialism as a realistic alternative to existing political problems. Others insist that the "worker and labor" mentality of socialism and liberal democratic theory cannot solve the issues of the day, since it presupposes the increased development of bureaucratic control in Washington. Consequently, the aims of classical socialism, wherein the power of the citizenry is heightened through economic advancement in organized labor, now becomes outdated because of the federal government's ability to adopt this force for its own political ends. The Vietnam war and its consequent support from labor only goes to prove the point of this latter group of radicals. The radicals who adopt socialism as their political platform and who also oppose the Vietnam war insist that the federal government is not really socialist in spite of the allegiance given it by some in the labor class of the society. To them the federal government is a political force bent on controlling the entire national populace through economic, legal, political, and military force. Their argument is that a socialist revolution in the political and economic sphere is the only salvation obtainable.

To some degree, then, there seems to be an ideological split in the radical movement. This fact is seldom recognized in the public press since most radicals are usually associated with socialist and Communist causes. This is completely misleading. Student radicalism has no one political platform, and this factor itself is the one thing that universally characterizes the movement. What we are dealing with in the student radical movement is a thoroughly American phenomenon. Although it is possible to find small groups within the New Left who identify themselves with Communists and other nationalist ideologies, it is incorrect to label the movement as guided by outside forces. On the contrary, we are witnessing a generation of students who want to be American but who do not want the imagery of Americanism.

It is the ethnocentrism of our national life that sticks in the throat of most young American radicals. As Marvin E. Gettleman, editor of *Vietnam: History, Documents and Opinions on a Major World Crisis*, has said, "A modern form of ethnocentrism is to deny the relevance, or even the existence, of the historical experience of peoples with which we become involved." Student radicals find that this factor has become one of the most unnecessary and embarrassing characteristics of modern American thinking. It feeds the generations of conservatives who want to insure their belief in our national superiority. And it disguises the intentions of those who would expand American industry and business throughout the world under the guise of development. Student radicals are therefore calling for an expresssion of national honesty based upon a realistic evaluation of the aims and interests of other peoples. Many adults insist that this is a totally unrealistic demand. But the question of which view is the more realistic has yet to be settled. The young radicals are willing to risk a great deal to prove that their moral argument is the only realistic and pragmatic stance to take. Ethnocentrism is a vice suited only to a nation that has little more with which to affirm itself. American ethnocentrism can be nothing less than imperialism once it is applied to international affairs. This is why radicals risk going to jail and suffering the possible loss of position and prestige. They do not want to identify themselves with the pridefulness of the strongest nation in the history of mankind.

5. Where Does the Campus End and the World Begin?

The place of the student radical on campus poses some interesting problems and provides a new perspective from which to examine the modern university. All of the issues that have taken them "off" the campus—civil rights work, Vietnam protest marches, rallies, and poverty projects—have tended to force many young radicals to take a hard look at their education.

In the process of raising questions about what they have learned both on and off campus, they have discovered that the whole problem of how one learns cannot be separated from what one learns. One student who spent an entire summer in Alabama pointed out, "I have learned more about the history of the South in three months than I ever would have learned in four years of college. And what I have learned about the South has also taught me much about the rest of this nation." In the particular case of this student, he learned while working with a Harvard graduate in history, a young Negro, teaching classes on subjects he had to spend hours preparing.

If the students found many of their classes back on the campus dull and uninteresting, they found that it didn't have to be that way. They had begun to develop a new attitude toward learning. It was learning through involvement. And though their experience was precisely what many academics back home wanted them to have, it nevertheless posed a serious challenge to the ways a great many courses are taught and it also posed a threat to the structures that tend to thwart the kinds of change these radicals are seeking.

Many young radicals began to adopt some of the ideals of Paul Goodman, whose books *Community of Scholars* and *Compulsory Mis-education* launched a headlong attack on the unnatural manner in which education through disciplines tends to thwart the free questioning and learning process so essential to basic higher education. Some students and faculty found themselves completely incapable of living in an atmosphere of fragmented and often irrelevant course materials. And so they attempted to set up their own Free Universities. There had been experiments in this direction before, but they never seemed to gather much support throughout the nation. Paul Goodman himself had already given a model for these "universities in exile." Essentially they were to be patterned on the medieval system, wherein students and faculty comprised the *collegium* and students determined the curriculum by seeking professors who would teach them what they wanted to learn. By the fall of 1965 a number of these Free Universities had appeared throughout the country, especially in California, New York, and the large Midwestern universities. In some instances, the content of the curriculum was strongly affected by political ideology, especially Marxist theory. And, in many cases, the influence of Hegel, Marx, and Freud seemed to determine many of the underlying philosophical assumptions. Although the enrollments in these Free Universities remains fairly small to date, their effect upon a number of campuses has been quite surprising.

Several universities, as well as a few smaller colleges, have recognized the dangers in discipline-oriented education. Harvard and the University of Chicago have long led the way in attempting to solve the problem of fragmented education through the creation of smaller and less rigid classes in the fields of the humanities and Western thought. But the impact of Sputnik in the fifties tended to force most of our larger universities to orient themselves toward meeting the asserted need of greater professional specialization in the sciences. By far the greatest amount of federal resources came to the departments of science and engineering; the humanities were often left to survive on their own. A few foundations attempted to remedy this condition, but the situation today has forced most of our major universities to work in league with the aims and purposes of the federal government, and particularly the Defense Department. Consequently, the student radicals often find themselves in direct opposition to their own universities because they cannot see a separation in the interests of the government and the universities. Complicating the matter is the fact that the government has become so used to dealing with the larger universities in getting them to provide services for the national interest, such as the case of the CIA and Michigan State University during the mid-fifties and the Institute for Cooperative Research in Chemical Warfare at Pennsylvania, that most universities seem to consider any effort to reverse this trend completely unrealistic. But that is precisely where the student protest is lodged. The Free University is an attempt to make a radical break with such influences.

On the other hand, there does seem to be something of a development in a few universities toward a curriculum revision in the direction of an issue-oriented education. How far this trend will go is yet to be seen. At least some academics are willing to make changes. But student radicals are cautious and even pessimistic about the results. The vast majority want to see a complete break with federal control, not to mention business and industry, to the point where our institutions of higher education cannot be used by any political or pseudo-political force for the perpetration of its own ends, no matter how much those ends may be deemed in the national interest. Although there are a great many faculty members throughout the country who agree with the student radicals on this point, attempts to join with the students and to effect significant changes in this direction remain insignificant to date.

Student radicals also know that the federal government is not the only outside interest the university must come to grips with. The neighborhoods around many of our larger campuses are little more than urban pockets of poverty, and the interests of the citizens who live in these areas often come into direct conflict with the aims of the university. This has been true at Chicago, New York, Philadelphia, Los Angeles, and most major cities throughout the country. While some institutions have had more success than others, the radicals have found themselves deeply involved in "block associations," doing much the same kind of work they did in Mississippi and Alabama—trying to help the poor master the means of getting what their constitutional rights have supposedly assured. In many cases, it is ironic that students who have no professional training in social work find themselves doing work that the professionals in their own universities ought to be doing. But some universities seem to have an aversion to utilizing their own talents in areas of concern to the neighborhoods that surround them. It is not uncommon to see a university hire some agency to do the work when there are literally hundreds of students and even professors who could do the job as well, and in many cases with far greater enthusiasm. Exactly why these universities seek other agencies and firms to carry out the aims of the university while ignoring the professionals in their own midsts is something of a mystery. In any case it is another example to the radicals of what has happened when universities are managed by individuals who believe that university life is, and ought to be, separated from the practical realities of the world around it. The fact that some of the universities are willing to permit students to tutor and teach the children in these sections of poverty, thus "gaining valuable experience in their learning," proves that the learning motif is still the guiding rule of thumb instead of the idea that universities should become institutions of practical service. The radicals, following the ideas of Paul Goodman, are convinced that education serves immediate and practical ends and does not, as some educators believe, provide a time and place wherein knowledge is allowed to build up for later practical solutions. The conflict over this point is one that seriously alienates the radicals from many of the academics who seem to fear that "excellence" will suffer if the practical problems of life intrude onto the campus. There is a serious doubt whether these academics will long be able to have their way. Outside forces have already profoundly affected the manner in which universities carry on their work. Thus the student radicals have begun to ask why the university is so prone to accept some of these government and business interests and not the interests of the poor and those who need the university the most.

6. A Guide to Radicalism on Campus

The student radical's relationships with other students and faculty are often determined by the activities we have mentioned. As was shown at Berkeley, the vast majority of students who consider themselves personally radical but do not actively work with some group or project have only a fleeting relationship with the visible radicals on campus. If a crowd gathers around some lecturer or speaker on a given subject of concern to the radicals, the makeup of that crowd may well have a sizable number of radical sympathizers present. There will also be the usual "jocks" —athletic types—a few ROTC members, and a fairly large number of interested bystanders. Even a few faculty members, one of whom may be giving the speech, will also be present, either as supporters or simply as listeners. But elsewhere on campus it is quite difficult to single out the radicals. In fact, the only thing that helps one who does not know the campus find the radical students is to hang around long enough to witness some visible show of protest. About the only other obvious sign of where the radicals are to be found will be at some table on campus, usually in a strategic spot, where materials relating to the concerns of radicals can be purchased.

This brings us to the most difficult part of trying to explain what the student radical movement really is. If one were to draw up a guide to student radicalism he would find that it is always incomplete and inevitably inaccurate. Radicalism is a movement in the most literal sense of the word. And as we have already tried to show, it is the issues which seem to tie the radicals together. In many cases a sense of community tends to grow out of those ties, but even here there is little constancy. And yet it is important to make certain distinctions among the various groups, though they do tend to give the impression of being united on the issues that count.

For example, one must be able to recognize a "Trotskyite." These are the militant Marxists who seem to be committed to immediate revolution and the socialist victory over capitalism. *Spartacist* is a journal of one of these Trotsky groups committed to the revolution. Other groups which fit into this camp would be the American Committee of the Fourth International; the Socialist Workers Party, founded by one of Leon Trotsky's American secretaries, James Cannon; and the Young Socialists' Alliance, which is the youth group of the Socialist Workers

Party. Much of the militant rhetoric that can be seen on fliers and pamphlets comes from groups like these, although they represent only a very small minority among the leftists. Their influence upon the student radicals is so small that it is practically unnecessary to mention them at all, except to give some attention to the fact that such groups do align themselves with the student radical movement. Consequently there may be a handful of Trots on campus, but they have little importance for the majority of radicals.

The problem of labeling any group Communist is another dilemma. Practically none of the student-run radical groups seeks to be known as Communist. The one avowedly Communist older group that has sponsored certain student groups is the Progressive Labor Party. But even the P.L. student groups tend to play down the Communist identification, mostly because the students in these groups have no interest in the cause of international communism. Some groups that have had tenuous relations with Progressive Labor, such as the May 2nd Movement (which no longer exists) and the American Liberation League, comprise another very small minority among radicals on campus. But when the FBI labeled the W. E. B. DuBois Club Communist in the spring of 1966, the general reaction of radical students was voiced by one young radical when he said, "Either the FBI doesn't know what it wants or how to get it, or else it needs another 'herring' to feed J. Edgar." Most student radicals associate with any number of so-called Communists and since a few Communists had taken over positions of leadership in a local chapter of the DuBois Club it seemed as if the FBI had wanted to "get" a few individuals by insisting that their leadership had made the club into a Communist organization. The vast majority of radicals, some of whom had been in the DuBois Club for a time, knew that the club was far less Communist than other groups that have yet to be approached by the government. The student radicals themselves certainly do not make the same associations that the FBI seems to have made in that special case. By and large, student radicals believe that any identification is pointless, since the real battles to be fought in this country leave little room to be concerned about international communism.

As we have pointed out, the "crazy" leftists, as one student radical calls them, have very little to do with the student radical movement. The Trots and the Communists seem to have their own little groups and they do attempt to infiltrate some of the larger campus protest groups. But, because of their exceedingly small influence among the students, they deserve no special attention.

When it comes to ad hoc committees and action groups we find the vast majority of student radicals moving in and out of one group into another. The term *socialist*, so widely used these days, does not adequately define many of these action organizations. Perhaps the Student Peace Union, local Independent Socialist Clubs, and the Student Socialist Union represent the only formal presence of socialists on any campus at any one time. Certainly, there are dozens of campus groups that hold to some socialist theory. But formal socialism and theoretical socialism are not precisely the same thing.

Nevertheless, it is the independent and ad hoc groups which seem to attract the largest number of student radicals on any given campus. Certainly, the various Independent Committees on Vietnam, which have several groups within their ranks, have been the most visible activist groups throughout the nation over the past two years. Then there are always a few pacifist organizations, such as the Committee for Non-Violent Action, and certain religious groups which support practically all protests against the war in Vietnam. But the one group that does not limit its concern to the Vietnam war, although there is very strong attention to the war, is the organization known as Students for a Democratic Society. This group is by far the most influential radical student organization on the campuses of our universities. Here we find a large group of students who represent the non-ideological aspects of the movement. SDS also demonstrates some of the clearest thinking regarding social action and change.

This is the group that stresses the over-all tendency of universities to feed the government's programs at the expense of self-determination. Their protest against the war in Vietnam is always related to the manner in which universities, business, industry, labor unions, and government interlock so as to thwart the democratic practice of a free society. Many of the leaders of SDS have become quite knowledgeable on the subjects of Southeast Asia, the CIA, what business groups are represented on the board of trustees of any given university; where the labor unions take their stands on the issue of war and peace, and why; where individuals in Congress stand on issues of international relations, the war in Vietnam, and basic issues of social change; and a host of interrelated problem areas.

SDS also seeks to face up to something the Trotsky and Communist groups do not seem to be coming to grips with—the problem of the inadequate manner in which this country has dealt with its own political principles. Many SDS adherents have begun seriously to rethink American political theory and practice. Paradoxically, many of the ideas that have had direct relevance to the "grand experiment," the American dream of democracy (which one might expect the nation to be concerned with) now become the existential concern of a group of radical students. Not that there are no other groups interested in many of these same matters; obviously there are many journals, and organizations like the Center for the Study of Democratic Institutions, Americans for Democratic Action, and the various groups which deal with legal, moral, and ethical aspects of American democracy. The fact that there are groups of student radicals who insist that the issues of today have gone beyond the old battles between capitalism and communism, who put forth arguments for the democratic advancement of all people, seems quite striking to many observers.

Many of these students have studied the *Federalist* papers, Jeffersonian democratic theory, and the whole area of relating the Constitution to modern life. They have diligently rethought many of the ideas of Hegel, Marx, and Freud, not for the purpose of betraying the principles of democracy but for the purpose of giving them a firmer philosophical and existential base. Many of them see quite clearly the fantastic impact of modern technology upon the age-old fears and burdens of man. Their programs regarding Vietnam, the government, the university, the economy, and the future of society are deeply rooted in the best political and social base available. One might readily call these young men and women the "radical democrats" of the day.

As noted earlier, much of what these student radicals have learned comes directly from their experiences in encountering the realities of our social and political life in civil rights work. On most of our nation's larger campuses we find chapters of CORE, the student side of the organization called the Congress of Racial Equality. This group was originally founded, like all other civil rights organizations, to fight the injustices of social, political, and economic segregation in the South. But CORE quickly realized that the problems the civil rights movement had to grapple with were not limited to the South. The problem of the Negro and other minority groups was a national one, as we all have come to realize in the past few years. In most cases it was directly related to the vast problem of poverty that honeycombs our entire culture. But when one seeks to examine why this country that has so much abundance and affluence also has such a staggering poverty and discrimination crisis, one begins to understand what the student radicals and the civil rights workers mean when they refer to the "system." The system in the South is easy for most Americans to see. The political machinery in Alabama and Mississippi, for example, is so geared to continuing segregation and discrimination that the only way Negroes have been able to help themselves is to fight the system, to replace it, or at least to democratize it. The system that works throughout the rest of the country is less visible to many Americans, but not to those who have had to fight it as well.

Examples of how this system works can be found in every city and every state in the Union. Fundamentally, it has to do with the manner in which large businesses and corporations seek to control the economic and political machinery at all levels of government. At the same time, the President of the United States, who represents the management of the overwhelming economic and financial resources of the nation, has the task of seeing that things run smoothly and in conjunction with his own aims in terms of the national interest. Added to this is the fact that individual businesses and corporations find themselves trying to do everything they can for the advancement of their industry (a traditional moral attitude in capitalism). But this means that the society must be highly controlled and managed, so as not to risk any one interest group's gaining too much power and thus controlling the market and the national economy.

By and large, the system seems to work. That is, until we come to those individuals who do not fit in. These are the unemployed, the poor, and the citizens who have no means of making their interests known. In the treatment of these individuals by the managers in Washington and the large cities, we see the system at its worst. For these poor citizens are asked to accept the society as it is, to believe in its aims and goals. But most of these aims and goals are symbolized by the images of large segregated institutions that ask not to be corrected or changed, not to be challenged or questioned, but to be accepted in their advancement toward greater control and power. The poverty program of the federal government seeks to enlarge and inculcate those goals, if not by direct intention at least by default.

The radical students who work for CORE know this to be characteristic of the system. They know what it is like to work with the poor and the segregated in attempting to help them organize themselves as a group that can challenge these vast interests in the country. They also know how insulting it is to be treated as individuals who "need" to be managed if they are to fit into the society. And many of the student radicals who work for CORE, but whose parents also represent the white and powerful interests of business and industry, find themselves bucking the same system which was created for their own benefit. All this is an education which they could have never received within the system.

Whether the system ends up by perpetuating poverty, using the military to drain off the uneducated and those unfortunate enough not to enter college, insuring the growth of the Defense Department and the space program, educating young men and women to feed into the larger corporations and industries of the nation, or simply brainwashing the American public that these practices must always continue, the fact remains that it is the one great enemy of the student radical movement. The system has to be fought, or—as one young SDS member said—"I don't want my life to be managed any longer. It was managed and controlled through a compulsory grade school, a compulsory high school, and now a compulsory college system. I guess, if I don't fight it, I'll find myself fighting the Viet Cong, and finally dying for the system. But I've learned one thing this last year. I don't have to do it any longer."

He learned that lesson while working for CORE and SDS. He could have also learned it while working for SCOPE, a project sponsored by the Southern Christian Leadership Council, which spends most of its time working on voter registration and social-action projects in the South. Or he could have learned it while working for SNCC, the Student Non-Violent Coordinating Committee, or maybe the Northern Student Movement, the Northern counterpart of SNCC. These groups work directly in the ghettos throughout the nation and train young people to fight the system while helping the citizens in these areas organize themselves in order to have their rights guaranteed. Much of the success of the Freedom Democratic party in Mississippi can be attributed to SNCC workers, not to mention all of the hard work that originally went into the voter-registration drives over the past few years.

From the handful of Trots and socialists on the one side all the way to the groups like SDS and the civil rights workers, the student radical movement has grown throughout the nation. It is practically impossible to estimate how many thousands of young people this entails. But one thing is certain. The movement has profoundly affected the universities and colleges which heretofore had known a relative peace and quiet among these students. Many of those who live and work on the campuses of our nation see something of great significance in the student radical movement. Faculty members have found themselves involved on the campus—and outside the classroom—as they never anticipated before. But one member of the university community who has been most concretely affected by the movement has been the campus minister. It is his role in relationship to the student radical movement that I would like to address myself to now.

7. *Allies in a Changing World*

The relationship between student radicals and campus ministers is in many respects a strange and often confusing association. On the one hand, it is completely understandable that individuals who share a common interest in issues should seek one another out and cultivate their common concerns. But when one looks at the traditional image that many clergy have become identified with and then compares this with the image that has followed the student radical movement, the contrast is a bit startling. But this is precisely the error of looking only to images. Images have the tendency to crystallize and oversimplify realities.

Actually the student radical movement has many of its roots in the same tradition as that from which campus clergy derive their present-day ministries. It is no secret that the clergy have always played a rather significant role in issues that affect the society as a whole. Those who complain that the clergy ought not to become involved in public issues such as politics, economics, poverty, war, and peace do not really understand the history of the ministry. In fact, the significance of American history cannot be completely explained without a continuous reference to the role played by the clergy. As Horace Walpole is supposed to have said during the American Revolution, while he was addressing Parliament, "Sister America has run off with a Presbyterian parson."

Equally, one cannot read the Old Testament without recognizing that modern rabbis are following in the steps of the prophets when they march for peace and demonstrate for equal rights. And many Catholic priests and nuns have a long and impressive history to back them up when they take a stand on certain political and moral issues of concern to the society.

All of this added to the recent stands taken by the Pope and the various councils of the Church and synagogues throughout the world completely refutes the argument that ministers who involve themselves in issues are out of step with their real mission. If anything, it is they who are the ones who give visible evidence of the most basic teachings of their faith. And this fact does not go unheeded by the student radicals throughout the nation.

But it would be completely misleading to assume from this that the radicals have responded to the clergy of the action-oriented side of religion by coming into the churches and temples as believers. The place of formal religion remains the same as it was before the radicals and the campus clergy discovered one another. This is completely understandable; in fact, there is some reason to believe that many campus ministers have learned from the radicals. But this too is as it ought to be. There is no place in the modern world for the old proselytizing spirit of the past, especially when the issues which confront us all demand understanding and acceptance of one another rather than attempts at converting one another.

The student radicals seem to recognize that this spirit of mutual understanding is what guides many campus clergy into involvement with the Left. Those who have labeled this as simply a devious attempt to seduce more students into the "faith" do not understand the motives of many of today's campus clergy.

But what are the motives of those churchmen who seek to identify themselves with students disaffected with our modern society? Certainly the reasons are quite different and distinct, considering the varied and unique backgrounds from which many ministers come. One of the fundamental motivations, however, is more conservative than liberal. But this should surprise no one. I am speaking of the fact that all the major religions have long and important traditions which have spoken of the very issues which concern us today. To take a stand on war and peace, for example, is certainly not new to the Judeo-Christian tradition. In fact, it would be quite liberal to assume that we have reached the point in history where the prophets and the New Testament have nothing to say to us regarding these matters. And those who ask their clergy to speak smooth things to them, "to cry peace when there is no peace," are actually asking them to betray their own authentic ministries. Even as we commented on the fact that it is the issues that seem to call forth the student radicals, so the same thing can be said of the activist campus ministers. This is not radical for clergy, no matter how many claim that this is the case. In fact, it is the most conservative step they could take. For it is an ancient Truth that commands them, and not some relative whim of their own imaginations.

Actually, even as we pointed out the interest within the student radical movement in the principles of the American Founding Fathers, so one must recognize the same kind of interest and concern among campus ministers who become involved in the movement. Yet this means that the interest is partially theological. It is quite important to understand that much of what motivates both the clergy and the student radicals grows out of the impact of the Judeo-Christian tradition. In many respects, it can be clearly seen that the young radicals are asking us to re-examine our own theological and moral history as we become more deeply involved in the issues of modern life.

When a group of students take a stand for free speech or self-determination they appear to be asking for something new. But it seems so only to those who have lost sight of their own historical values. What is new in that kind of protest is the developing awareness of this problem among the young. Students have not been used to this kind of direct action for a very long time. This is especially true in this country. Of course, what we are beginning to realize is the fact that modern society has created a problem called adolescence, which it has yet to understand how to deal with. In the past there wasn't such a phenomenon because most children simply went from childhood into adulthood much faster than today. The labor- and toil-oriented world of our grandfathers solved the problem by not permitting it to exist. A young man or woman made the shift from one place in life to another because it was necessary to do so. The society needed them.

But today we are experiencing the profoundly disturbing reality that our culture increasingly does not need its young people. That is, unless we need them to fight our wars or perform such other duties as their youth seems amenable to. This can be shown to be true in a vast majority of situations. Perhaps the most obvious area of concern to many is the problem of education itself. Seymour Melman, author of *Our Depleted Society* has said:

Children are sensitive to the adult community's indifference to their education, and they respond by quitting, in large numbers, the schools where overcrowding, over-large classes, and poor facilities indicate to them how little the community cares for them. One-third of the students attaining the fifth grade have not been completing high school. Drop-outs along the way number one million per year. Some time after the drop-out rate and the drop-outs' subsequent unemployment began to be a national scandal, studies were made of the characteristics of the drop-out students. It was discovered that half of the drop-outs had IQ's of average or greater than average capacity, and that 80 per cent of them would have been capable of absorbing a high-school education or pushing work at the college level.

If one does not think that the student radicals are familiar with such facts as these he simply does not know how informed they really are. Many of the radicals in the movement are dropouts themselves. This is not because they are poor students or incapable of doing the work; it is because they want to be treated as adults. Adulthood seems to be the only place where one can be given any serious attention, and if they don't find it there they discover that they have to demand it.

In other words, the period we have labeled *adolescence* is a monstrosity that ought not to exist in the manner in which it is cultivated in this society. It is basically insulting to our young people, and many of them are showing us how they feel about it. Some react with violence, the return to childish rebellion. But these are the young people who have a serious dependency problem. They are forced to react to the adult world showing their emotional dependence and their frustration in violent and destructive behavior. These young people are the rebels. They come from all walks of life; they treat adolescence as a waste of time, which they intend to waste at every turn. Many of them who are fortunate enough to enter college waste that time also. Because there are so many of them, it is often true that the structures of college administrations, not to mention the kinds of courses taught, are geared to prolonging and even feeding this frustrated and rebellious spirit. The classic example of this is the military school and the introduction of military training in most of our colleges and universities. This only betrays the fact that most adults seem to believe that adolescence is a period that must be forcibly structured because it is so explosive.

On the other hand, we find radicals who are asking that these structured and ordered processes be humanized, that educators take seriously the natural questioning spirit of youth. There is a profoundly different interpretation that the radicals give to the problem of adolescence. They ask that it be ignored wherever and whenever possible. They demand that the society take youth seriously and begin to share some of the wealth being wasted on war and space, that it be redirected to the purposes of serving youth instead of structuring it. And most of them find that they have a large and impressive amount of professional support on their side. It is also true that many campus ministers come to their aid at this point. Instead of siding with the authorities, who are uneasy about their students (the radicals have learned how to use the public relations office as a barometer of the universities' capacity for tension), the campus clergy find themselves aligned with the radicals. Part of this has to do with the fact that the radicals respond honestly and supportively to the attempts of the ministers to be relevant to the needs of the university. But a far more important reason is that the radicals represent something that is a fundamentally and thoroughly new challenge to the church. They simply do not fit into the old theological and structural categories that the church anticipated a generation ago.

8. What the Radical Students Have Taught Us

On the one hand, the young radicals have all the interest and concern that one would expect from a committed Christian. Yet they ask none of the traditional questions and refuse to accept any of the traditional answers that have marked the dialogues between the church and the university in the past. In fact, they often tend to raise the kind of questions that force theology to become radical in order for the two to be able to communicate meaningfully. And this one factor, plus the other fantastic challenges of technology, poverty, abundance, and the changing spirit within the church, tends to influence the campus minister into becoming even more radical than he had anticipated. It is for this reason that much of the Death-of-God theology—which the public press seems to want to limit to a small handful of radical theologians—really has much of its origin in the relationship between the campus minister and the radical students.

At the heart of this development is the interesting manner in which a new theology of man, instead of a theology of God, begins to be developed. In many ways the radical students themselves represent the *man* that traditional, and especially neo-orthodox, theology does not understand. One cannot speak to them of sin and make much sense. Nor can one explain the meaning of Providence in the face of the older generations' refusal to take the responsibility for their own world. Providence means to a radical that someone is trying to rationalize away his responsibility for the world in which he lives. Sin means that a man is blameworthy to God instead of to himself and the community of human beings which surrounds him. This is what the radicals refuse to accept, and they are quite right. Consequently, an appropriate kind of language for dealing with this attitude toward reality is the radical theology of theologians like William Hamilton, Thomas Altizer, Harvey Cox, and even men like Robert Theobald, Marshall McLuhan, Kenneth Boulding, and Buckminster Fuller (not theologians but men who do present theological problems for the radical theologians).

Since radical theology is still in the formative stages, much of what the campus minister finds himself doing, in terms of his theological teaching and study, is almost completely in the process of formulation. This is partly a reflection of the drastic innovations affecting the whole of society today. But the student radical himself poses for the campus minister one of the most significant innovations in the modern world. As suggested, the old theological concepts of sin and Providence that served at one time as meaningful terms describing the problem of man and the meaning of history can no longer speak to the radicals. Any serious look at the young men and women who make up the movement makes it clear that we are dealing with individuals who understand man's problem, as well as their own, in terms of arrogance and laziness, not of sin and sickness of the soul. In fact, these latter terms describe the old Marxist and neo-orthodox "condition of man," which has proved the very frame of reference of liberals who today have no real answers to the problems of necessary and rapid change. The impotence of liberalism has now met with the abounding energy and profoundly significant optimism of radicalism, and the liberals do not know how to respond. But those campus clergy who live with these radicals have discovered that that same neo-orthodoxy not only cannot continue to be used on campus, but it has become an albatross around the neck.

One of the forms that radical change in theology is taking is to be found in the Death-of-God theology and the secular-city motif of modern religious experience. Whereas many individuals feel themselves completely involved in the secular world of mass communications and rapid change, the campus confronts the university pastor with the same reality, only heightened to a far greater degree by the fact that many of the innovations in contemporary society have their origins in the university community. However, this is only partially true. In one sense it is possible to see the university as one of the last bastions of resistance against the fantastic changes taking place within our society. Much of the technological advance within our society is not meaningfully or responsibly being faced up to in many of our universities and colleges. Instead of an overwhelming support for some of the practical effect this could have for education, there seems to be a cautiousness that almost appears to be intended to impede change. The classic example of this can be found in the experience of learning to think. Since most larger universities consider themselves "knowledge factories" and "banks" wherein the information of the world is stored, the process of education ends up with a very high priority placed upon the incorporation and regurgitation of that knowledge. Student radicals forced to go through this experience naturally revolt and demand that the university return to the original task of teaching students how to think and make sense of all this information.

When this is not done, some of them discover that the local campus minister, who often agrees with their aims for education, is a fairly good example of one who is committed to the experience of thinking. His techniques do not demand that a student sit through long and continuous seminars that disseminate routine information. Instead he asks that information be examined and that new and useful ideas be developed regarding this information. It may involve economics, politics, religion, literature, science, sociology, or a host of related subjects. One thing is certain—the goal is not to master large amounts of information that are not really information but content and can easily be obtained with the help of a speed-reading course. Learning to think about it is something else. This is one of the things the campus minister asks for. And the response of many students, especially radicals, is positive. By default, the campus ministry finds itself involved in filling a vacuum that ought not exist. But, unfortunately, it does exist to a far greater degree than most universities like to admit.

Another aspect of this learning to think (and it must be made clear that every university has its minority of scholars who are committed to learning and thinking) is reflected in the way students react to the challenge of learning, symbolized in their continuous movement from one learning experience to another. If universities permitted them, the young radicals would probably find themselves going to at least a dozen classes, off and on, throughout the semester. They would move where the ideas and the knowledge are flowing most freely. Of course, no administrator would ever consider such a nonstructured attitude to learning very manageable. He could not be certain of what the students are learning. And if he cannot be certain of what they are learning, he cannot be sure they have learned anything at all. He also would find it impossible to say to some business firm, or perhaps the Selective Service System, exactly where a particular student is within the structure of the university. But, of course, that presupposes that it is important to exercise controls over what one learns. And this is precisely where students find themselves at odds with university administrations. The student finds controls where he wants freedom, and he finds limits where he wants to choose for himself. This is the story of the modern university.

9. The Future Is Our Judge

Obviously this conflict over the basic aims and practices of education in our society, the conflict between managed education with its attendant problems and the interpersonal freedom-to-learn-how-to-think type of education that the radicals insist upon, reflects a fundamental point of contention over not so much what should go on in a university today as over what will happen if the present pattern continues.

In a sense (and many of them are completely aware of it) the radicals are arguing for a style of education that carries with it certain political overtones. They are insisting that no society can call itself free, as we have tried to do for so many years, while permitting our means of educating the young to be predetermined by those who have an interest in what one learns. That interest can, and must, be the responsibility solely of the student. The guidance he needs can be left at a minimum, if one presupposes that guidance is the proper concern of the teacher and not the administrator. But since the role of the teacher is quite secondary in our system of higher education, because of the role education plays in serving the interests of the government, business, and industry, this latter aim of the radicals immediately places them at odds with those ends.

The campus minister finds himself theologically, and therefore existentially, in complete agreement with the radicals once again. This is particularly true of those clergy who themselves are radicals in theology. Any serious evaluation of the impact that technology is having upon our society, an impact that cannot help growing by even more fantastic leaps and bounds, must take note of kinds of change the old theological notions of the last generation cannot continue to serve. For example, when the radical theologians affirm the death of God, one of the things they are saying to our universities is that man must be trusted. This, of course, means that the student is going to have to be trusted. And the attitude with which he is judged and corrected will have to come from elsewhere than the traditional "expert versus novice" assumptions of most institutions of higher learning.

In the context, then, of the campus ministers' understanding of the Gospel, or the *kerygma*—as it is called in the New Testament—we find a stance toward the future with much to say to the university and the student in the present. In the first century, that future was pictured as the "coming of the Kingdom of God on earth." Today, anyone who looks for the Kingdom of God "coming on the clouds of Glory" (and that means in the future which is close enough to see, but not so close as to be called the present) stands in radical judgment over the ways in which the present time is lived by those who witness the "coming future." In other words, if one sees the technological revolution coming in upon modern man with the rapidity of today, and one does not feel judged and freed to act by responding openly to that future, he has written his own death certificate. This also means that if our managed society is permitted to continue and the advances of technology continue as they will, we have begun to inhabit a world that will be ruled by managers. And for whatever means they seek to use the tools of modern technology, history will be completely in their hands to determine.

The young radicals, who see this possibility (and present reality to some degree) therefore find themselves completely identified with those who have the most to lose in that event. They stand with the poor, the minorities, and the foreigners who suffer because of their disadvantage in not being a part of the "abundant society." In Vietnam, the poor (led by Communist nationals) began to fight against the French colonialists, only to find themselves later fighting Americans who think that Communism must be stopped—no matter who gets killed, or how many, or how. The symbol of this conflict is the contrast between the multibillion-dollar techniques of warfare used by the Americans and the crude but skillful techniques of those who have little more than the wish to determine their own lives. The radicals see in this, rightly, the same contrast that can be found in the rest of our society—between those who ask to be free to determine their own lives and those who insist that they must be managed by those who know better. Theologically and morally, the campus minister finds himself standing on the side of those who demand freedom.

If this means that the campus clergyman should stand up and speak out—and it usually does—this is what will happen. If it means that he is called upon to provide means by which students are free to think and study materials outside their curriculum, this is what will happen. If it also means that certain action must be taken to change the managed society into a freer society, this too must be tried. All in all, this is why the campus pastor finds himself involved with student radicals.

What is the future relationship between the student radical and the campus minister? It would appear that the involved and concerned university pastor has begun to create a place for himself in the university which makes him a valuable colleague for the student radicals. As a person committed to the kinds of change demanded by the world we live in today, and as a result of his theological and personal training, the campus minister finds himself involved in ways that he could never have anticipated a decade ago. He has found colleagues and associates on and off campus who challenge his ministry and demand his participation in the struggle for change that is becoming universal.

It is also true that since the radical theology that is only now in its developmental stages faces an exciting and meaningful future, the association with radicalism on and off campus cannot help growing. Whatever changes take place in the university, the campus minister is bound to be involved. Whatever changes take place in the society, as a result of the fact that the traditional barriers between university and society are breaking down, the campus pastor is also going to find himself engaged. This engagement cannot help paralleling the relationship he has with the radicals on campus. The things that need to be done in our society, the things that need to be said, cannot be done and said without the campus minister being at the very heart of the issues.

Obviously, one should not assume from this that all campus ministers who work with the student radicals are themselves radicals, theologically or otherwise. Some find themselves involved with the young radicals because they seem the most exciting and relevant groups on campus. Others relate to them because there is a natural tie of interest in social issues. Still others find in the student radicals something of a modern-day continuation of the movements of social action that were originally a part of the Judeo-Christian tradition.

But the campus minister who now begins to think of himself as a radical is something of a new breed. Of course, certain aspects of any religious point of view can be called radical. The very nature of the Judeo-Christian tradition betrays a "radical" stance toward the world. But this traditional radicalism only acts as a kind of springboard for the style of radicalism that some campus clergy find themselves adopting today.

One form of this radical attitude can be found in what appears a most presumptuous position many campus ministers have taken regarding the very business of the university itself. This is partly due to the situation in which the campus clergyman finds himself, since he often takes stands on issues that directly relate to the university. If, for example, the radical campus minister sees that a large university practices a system of "educating" that either ignores or overlooks certain vital issues he feels it must deal with, then he becomes involved in confronting that institution with its own aims and practices. This may involve anything from outright criticism of the university's practices with regard to the local neighborhood, the nature of the curriculum, the stance of the university toward the Vietnam war, the relationship of the university to outside interest groups all the way to specific practices of certain officials with regard to individual students.

As I have pointed out before, another example of radical presumptuousness can be found whenever the campus minister finds himself filling a void the university ought to be stepping into. The most obvious area where this can be found (and there are always many exceptions) is in the concern for teaching students how to think instead of demanding the incorporation of massive and often insignificant data. However, this does not mean that the radical campus pastor assumes he is alone in this task; that would be the worst kind of arrogance. It would also be stupid and would reveal a serious lack of awareness about the campus itself. Every large campus has its share of excellent professors who are profoundly committed to the problem of teaching students how to think. But to assume that this means that the university has really faced up to this problem is to give the university too much credit. No modern university that attempts to gratify all the demands made upon it by influential groups outside the campus can be expected to be radically committed to the quality of thinking that should take place in the student body. But this is precisely what the radical campus minister finds himself committed to. The conflict then becomes almost inevitable.

But why does the radical minister interest himself in such an academic problem as learning how to think? Why does he not limit himself to areas of theological and ethical concern? The answer to this must always be that the problem of thinking is inextricably bound up with theology and ethics. If a student is permitted to take any course in a modern curriculum in which he is not taught to think of the significance or the meaning of what he is learning, he is being merely programmed instead of educated. And any brief glance at the manner in which many of our larger universities and colleges carry on their systems of guiding students through four years of academia forces one to realize that learning to think has become a luxury many cannot afford; the tangible goals of a degree and a job have become far more important. Theologically and ethically the campus minister tries to become something of a stumbling block to that mechanical process.

Finally, if the radical university pastor attempts to challenge that process, his ministry on campus will often set human beings over against institutional aims. Many campus ministers have begun to realize that the university community is still a human community with human problems. Although the academic world still insists that its reason for being is intellectual (and one must fully appreciate this fact), the university pastor cannot escape meeting the human needs of the academic community.

While the university seems to be racing headlong into a world of specialists, the campus minister has his work cut out for him. The task of helping the community deal with ever-present moral, ethical, and theological dilemmas remains a constant task.

To a certain degree, we have yet to understand what qualifications a campus pastor really needs to do his job best. But if he is competent in listening and learning, if he can be articulate in expressing his own ideas, and if he can love those to whom he ministers, he has a task that ought to last as long as there remain institutions called universities.

Vatican II
and the Newman Apostolate

JAMES EDWARD REA

J ust over fifty years ago at the now long-defunct Catholic Summer School of Cliff Haven, New York, there was held the first general meeting of what was then known as the Federation of Catholic College Students. This organization, bringing together Catholic faculty, students, and chaplains, was later to become the National Newman Club Federation, and, within the past few years, the National Newman Apostolate.

During the early decades of our century it was unusual for a man and still more unusual for a woman to go to college. For Catholic men and women the experience was very rare indeed. With notable exceptions, those of college age were of the first or second generation of working-class parents and were fortunate if they were able to finish high school before going to work themselves. The Catholic colleges of those days were relatively expensive for the middle-class families they were intended to serve, and there were very few scholarships available from either private or public funds. And, for a variety of reasons which have been analyzed over and over again in other places, Catholic students were given little or no encouragement to take advantage of the relatively inexpensive public and state colleges.

Half a century later the picture has changed completely. Now it is almost the normal thing, among Catholics as among others, for both young men and young women to go to college, provided they can measure up to academic standards. In order to meet the demand, Catholic colleges have multiplied and expanded, to the extent that at the moment they are caring for some four hundred thousand students throughout the country. That this has been a daring venture in higher education on the part of the Church—perhaps incomparable—cannot be denied. It becomes even more impressive when one realizes that the entire enterprise is made possible through the dedication of nearly nine thousand priests and religious who have devoted their lives to it. Yet the truth remains that this venture, daring and impressive as it may be, is able to serve only about 40 per cent of the entire Catholic student population. Moreover, as the "college boom" grows, despite whatever efforts the Church may make, the percentage is bound to shrink significantly as we pass from the 1960s into the 1970s.

Increasing numbers of Catholic students for recognizable economic reasons (there are no free Catholic colleges and the number of scholarships is few), are taking advantage of the relatively inexpensive tax-supported colleges on the state and municipal level. Others, including some of the most able graduates of our high schools and prep schools, are matriculating in the private non-Catholic colleges. For even though these institutions, in common with Catholic colleges, are threatened by the growth of public education, they are able to offer much more extensive scholarship aid than Catholic colleges can provide. The better students can qualify for such aid, and, as a result, take advantage of the broader curricula and greater opportunities for specialization that the Ivy League Colleges and their counterparts throughout the country can provide.

All these developments have grave implications for the Catholic college of today and tomorrow. As many of our prominent educational leaders realize, the need for expansion must not take precedence over the need for excellence in our system of higher education. But they bear even graver implications for the ever-growing Catholic population on the secular campuses. The present situation has not come into existence overnight. It is the result of a gradual process that has been developing ever since the close of the Second World War. For too long a time, as it seems to us who have been engaged in the Catholic ministry on campus, all this has gone seemingly unnoticed. But in recent years there have been signs that the Church in the United States has begun to take serious and official note of the revolution that is taking place. For the Catholic ministry to higher education must, if it is to be a reality, exist not just for 30 or 40 per cent of our college students, but for the other 60 or 70 per cent as well.

A great step forward was made by the bishops of the whole country a few years ago when they designated the Newman Movement an official Apostolate. Previous to that the bishops had authorized the National Newman Foundation a vehicle for public relations and fund-raising for the Newman cause. This has been followed, and in some cases had been preceded locally, by the recognition of foundations attached to individual colleges, or in the case of the Cardinal Newman Foundation of New York, attached to individual dioceses. In recent years also, the National Catholic Education Association has welcomed Newman centers throughout the country to institutional membership on the basis of their educational programs. These have all been helpful and hopeful developments.

Most significant, however, is the establishment of the Newman Apostolate, major credit for which must go to the Most Reverend Paul J. Hallinan, now Archbishop of Atlanta but formerly Episcopal Moderator of the Newman Federation and, for many years, a Newman chaplain in his home diocese of Cleveland. An Apostolate, in the understanding of the Church, is a gathering-together in organization of all those who, from one position or another, have concern for a particular work of the Church. The work in this case is the witness of the Church to the secular campus. Previously the work was thought of as involving only students with their chaplains and as directed toward a "holding action" of preserving the faith. According to the emerging concept, the work is seen as the concern not only of the students, but also of faculty and staff, of alumni, of the various foundations, and of Newman chaplains with their religious or lay associates all working together in a mission of witness to the secular campus.

But there remains a fundamental problem: What is the theory of the Newman Apostolate? What is its philosophy? What its theology? Certainly a movement that has taken its name and inspiration from John Henry Newman himself ought by this time to have constructed some philosophy and theology that would serve to motivate and direct its purpose. Yet I fear that these are still wanting. These pages are aimed not at solving this problem, but at suggesting some guidelines in the direction of a solution.

The ghettolike program of the older Newman clubs, which emphasized—on almost an equal basis—the religious, the social, and the intellectual for the purpose of uniting Catholic students apart from, outside of, and virtually over against the college community itself, is no longer either possible or practicable. It remains a temptation, however, since in the face of inadequate facilities it is the easiest program and the least disturbing to the quiescent conscience. But whoever tries it today will find that it will not work; in fact it will produce effects the reverse of those intended.

The world of today is not the world of fifty or even twenty-five years ago. And the secular college of today is a mirror of the world as it is, not as it was. Just as the Church as a whole is seeking to make itself contemporaneous with this world of today, so must the Newman Apostolate make itself contemporaneous with its campus world. It must become relevant, and to become relevant it must change its image. But, as with the Church (though not to the same degree), the change must be in terms of development, not in terms of the denial of its own basic traditions.

In this context, I think, we can turn to what some have described as the most significant religious event of our day, the Second Council of the Vatican. Except in one place, the Fathers of the Council did not explicitly avert to the problem we are considering. The lone exception occurs in a little-known and less-publicized "Declaration on Christian Education," which was passed by the bishops and promulgated by Pope Paul VI October 28, 1965. The purpose of the document is to restate the universal right to education in general and to Christian education for Christian children, as well as to redefine the responsibilities of parents, Church, and state in this regard. One section (7) deals with the problem of religious education in schools that are not Catholic:

Feeling very keenly the weighty responsibility of diligently caring for the moral and religious education of all her children, the Church must be present with her own special affection and help for the great number who are being trained in schools that are not Catholic. This is possible by the witness of the lives of those who teach and direct them, by the apostolic action of fellow students, but especially in the ministry of priests and laymen who give them the doctrine of salvation in a way suited to their age and circumstances and provide spiritual aid in every way the times and conditions allow.

The Church reminds parents of the duty that is theirs to arrange and even demand that their children be able to enjoy these aids and advance in their Christian formation to a degree that is abreast of their development in secular subjects. Therefore, the Church esteems highly those civil authorities and societies which, bearing in mind the pluralism of contemporary society and respecting religious freedom, assist families so that the education of their children can be imparted in all schools according to the individual moral and religious principles of the families.

The pastoral tone of this statement is obvious, as is also the fact that it relates principally to conditions prevailing on the elementary and secondary levels of education. Consequently it emphasizes the concern of the Church on one hand and parental responsibilities and rights on the other. The objective of religious education, however, is clearly stated and this obviously applies also on higher levels: that the students "advance in their Christian formation to a degree that is abreast of their development in secular subjects." This, even on the higher levels, is to be brought about "by the witness of the lives of those who teach and direct them, by the apostolic action of their fellow students, but especially by the ministry of priests and laymen" who have this as their specific goal.

All this, I submit, belongs to what I have called the basic traditions of the Newman movement. It is, however, on the college level, the right and responsibility of the student himself to "keep abreast." It is he who must realize the need and take advantage of whatever aids are provided him. It is chiefly the responsibility of the Church to provide those aids and they must be provided to an ever-increasing degree. It seems to me, however, that this responsibility rests not only on the Church but also on the administration of secular colleges and universities. There is much that should be provided in the average college curriculum that is actually ignored. On the part of the university this is not a religious responsibility but a cultural and intellectual one. To their credit, let it be said that there are increasing numbers of state and private universities that are enlarging their faculties to include competent representatives of the Catholic as well as other religious traditions. Other colleges will accept credits for courses given in special institutes set up by the religious bodies themselves.

I trust that this suggestion does not sound unecumenical. I do not intend it in that spirit. The fact is that pluralism, as the Fathers of the Council say, is with us, and education in a pluralistic society can take two directions. It can ignore all matters that divide and concentrate only on those that, on some basis, unite. Or it can seek to treat even of divisive matters in as fair and effective a manner as possible, in the trust that, after all, knowledge is a better base for unity than ignorance. Following the former method has led in secular and private education to the development of the religious illiterate who, precisely because he is a religious illiterate, finds himself ignorant also of many of the influences, perhaps the most important influences, that have shaped our world. To be fair I must admit also that the confinement of education about religion to religious educators operating within their own traditions has seemed to develop in many instances biased religious literates whose interpretation of the influences that have shaped the world is warped. But there is something wrong with an educational tradition that ignores whole areas of life and history because they are not patient of a monolithic interpretation. And this, I feel, is the effect of the attempted neutrality of so much American education at every level.

It is preferable to treat fairly and effectively of the matters that divide, in the trust, as I said above, that knowledge will eventually prove a better basis for understanding than ignorance. This is the true ecumenical spirit: not to ignore differences and act as though they did not exist, but to face them in a mutual attempt at understanding with, of course, charity and love. Religion may, as in the mind of Harvey Cox, be irrelevant to the *technopolis* of today (or is it tomorrow?). But for those of us (and there are many left) who still live in the *town*, if not in the *tribe*, and still maintain our religious commitments, the past remains relevant. As for those who are already living in *technopolis*, a glance back would do them no harm. The pillar of salt has been fairly well demythologized.

Before moving on to the more subtle and far-reaching elements in the teaching of Vatican II, allow me for a moment to point out one facet of the statement on Christian education cited above. The reader will note that the underlying supposition of the Fathers is that religious education is a subject in much the same way as secular subjects. This means that religion is presumed to have a certain intellectual content. This the Christian Church has taken as a matter of fact ever since Paul and John began to theologize. The Church sets great store in the meditations and writings of her fathers, her doctors, her theologians. Perhaps the reason for this was best stated by Cardinal Newman, who wrote of faith that it is "an act of the mind, whose object is truth and whose result is knowledge." To the Church, the commitment of faith is never altogether blind, nor does it result merely in wishful thinking. She regards the defined propositions of the faith as found in the creeds and elsewhere as important because they constitute an attempt to express understandably the content of her faith. She does not deny that these propositions are patient of improvement or that they can be couched in language that is increasingly more relevant and meaningful to changing times. Furthermore, she understands, with Thomas Aquinas, that the knowledge that faith brings has as its term, not the proposition itself but the supernatural reality that the proposition inadequately seeks to express. Religion is therefore broader than and goes beyond its intellectual apprehension and expression. Nevertheless, insofar as it can be expressed and apprehended, it is both learnable and teachable. Otherwise it is mere superstition!

We have emphasized the fact that higher education for all Catholics in Catholic institutions is a fast-fading dream. As a result, we must ask the question: How is the Catholic student (and the Church) to cope with the problem of the Catholic student on the secular campus? The Fathers of the Council have (I think) provided some material for an answer. For one thing, they have given the word *secular* an honorable connotation. Until very recently, the term *secular* applied to an institution of learning in Catholic circles carried a pejorative meaning. It meant not a-Catholic but anti-Catholic. In this there are Jansenistic overtones. The fact is, as the Fathers of the Council point out, that the word *secular* refers simply to the temporal order as distinguished from eternal destiny. In the words of the Decree on the Lay Apostolate (November 18, 1965), the temporal order has its own rights:

All those things which make up the temporal order, namely, the blessings of life and family, culture, economic matters, the arts and professions, the institutions of the civic community, international relations, and other matters of this kind, and their development and progress, not only aid in the attainment of man's ultimate goal but also possess their own intrinsic value. [II, 7]

Certainly, colleges and universities are included in the "institutions of the civic community." Secular learning includes all the arts, sciences, and skills that are not specifically theological. It is the key to the development of the temporal order—which, in itself, is part of God's plan from the beginning. The divine command of Genesis placed on the hands and mind of man the onus of perfecting the world and all that is in it. Each single advance of discovery or adaptation marks a step in the unfolding of God's own plan. For it was He who chose man to rule the universe. The notion that man in his humanity falls into insignificance or is buried in meaninglessness as a result of his own creative discoveries and adaptations is an absurdity. His genius and his inventiveness in the temporal order are only proof that he is, indeed, made in the image of God.

Granting that God had more in mind for man than the subjugation of nature—that He intended ultimately to raise man, and nature with him, to a new grace and dignity in Christ, it remains, in the words of the decree, that:

This design, however, not only does not deprive the temporal order of its independence, its own goals, laws, supports and importance for human welfare, but rather perfects the temporal order in its own intrinsic strength and excellence and puts it on a level with man's whole vocation on earth. [II, 7]

The *saeculum*, then, is not to be avoided or escaped from; it is to be cultivated. Secular learning as well as religious knowledge has "its independence, its own goals, laws, supports and importance. . . ." The cause of the sacred as well as sacred learning is ill-served wherever it impinges upon the independence of the secular or seeks to impose its own goals upon it. (The reverse process, of course, would mean the utter destruction of the sacred.) But this process, while taking the secular out of perspective, also tends to distort the image of the sacred. Secular and sacred learning, remaining independent of each other, each seeking the implementation of its own purposes, are intended to provide man with the tentatives and the conclusions that will enable him to pursue his "whole vocation."

Religious thinkers in the past have been too prone to ignore the gigantic contributions purely secular learning has made to theology. Today only the laggards are so inclined. Who can ignore, for example, the impact made by such diverse sciences as anthropology, archeology, ancient history, linguistics, and comparative literature upon our understanding of the Scriptures in which we find the sources of our belief? Who can deny the value of the findings of the relatively modern sciences of sociology and psychology for the application of the Church's inherently unchanging moral and ethical values in a changing world? The discoveries of these and many other secular sciences, taken objectively on their own terms, enable theology to advance from year to year and from day to day, even as they enlarge everyman's knowledge of the temporal order in which he lives. It is God's will that both sacred and secular learning contribute to our understanding of His own self-revelation, yet each in its proper way.

Secular thinkers (I use the term in its older pejorative sense) in the past have tended either to ignore or to denigrate religious values, as though this were a conclusion of their respective sciences. Today, however, as they search with greater objectivity and with a deeper awareness of the complexities of their fields, they are more and more inclined, if not to accept, at least to respect the great religious traditions and the role they have played in molding contemporary man. By this I do not mean that there is more belief as such in the academic community; there is probably much less than even a generation ago. But his very objectivity has freed the secular thinker from the prisons of nineteenth-century religious liberalism while also enabling the religious thinker to pursue his goals with a newfound freedom. Granted, there are pockets remaining on virtually every college campus of old-style secular thinking, just as in denominational colleges there remain pockets of old-style religious thinking, but the over-all picture is one of greater openness on both sides. The possibility of collaboration between secular and religious thinkers is real and genuine.

For example, during the past year, my office in cooperation with our Graduate Newman Association sponsored a lecture by Dr. Isidor Rabi, the Nobel Prize physicist. We were aware beforehand that his ideas about religion had little or nothing in common with ours. One thing we did know: he was as much concerned as we with the frightening prospect of the dehumanization of man in the age of atoms and automation. The result was an illuminating, although in part frustrating, exchange of ideas. Conversely, Columbia's religious counselors as a group were invited by members of the faculty of the Engineering School to participate in a series of programs aimed at enabling their students to work toward a set of values that would transcend those of the merely professional order. A similar program is in prospect for the School of General Studies.

One more example from my own experience: Many years ago Columbia pioneered a program in what is called Contemporary Civilization—a program later adopted or adapted in many universities throughout the country. It centers about a source book containing selections roughly in chronological order from the writers, teachers, and thinkers who over the centuries have influenced to a greater or less degree the course of history. The original editors had included just one short selection from the works of Thomas Aquinas—a page or so of his thinking about usury. But the recently revised edition contains relatively substantial excerpts from his philosophical and theological writings that have contributed to the intellectual and cultural development of modern man—another indication of the growing objectivity of the secular academic community.

In spite of the fact that there are many who criticize courses in contemporary civilization or surveys of the humanities as cultural grab-bags, I feel they do have a positive value. This rather uncritical juxtaposition of sacred and secular thinking and philosophy is for many students—Catholic and non-Catholic—their first and often their only exposure to any kind of religious thinking or philosophy. For some it comes as a shock that it is possible or worthwhile to think about the sacred or to reason about it. In the hands of an instructor (not necessarily a believer) who can put these thinkers and their thoughts in a realistic social and cultural context, such courses can be a revelation to the students and often cause a revolution in their lives. But where, as all too often happens, the instructor does not possess this ability, the student is encouraged, not to open his mind to the treasures of the past and to make them part of his own intellectual store, but to use his unformed mid-twentieth-century mind as a kind of sieve through which to strain the golden thought that is our heritage. From this kind of sifting, all that can emerge is what fits into the categories of his immaturity; his treasure is fool's gold indeed. In this process, while his secular heritage is impaired, his sacred heritage quite understandably suffers even more. At any rate, under the best circumstances, courses in contemporary civilization and in the humanities cannot provide the student the integrated view of the secular and the sacred that we call wisdom. Nor can this be accomplished in any great measure by the introduction into the curriculum of the courses in religious thought mentioned earlier, desirable though such courses are.

It is significant that when the Church founded the great universities of the West during the Middle Ages, she established them not as seminaries or schools of theology, but as genuine "universities." Just as in the lower schools the *trivium* and *quadrivium* had to be mastered, so on the university level knowledge, both secular and sacred, was transmitted, and all truth—both secular and sacred—was pursued. True, theology was regarded as the "queen of the sciences," and philosophy as her handmaid. But the secular sciences also had their place of honor and as a general rule, their independence. Who can measure the value of the transmission and augmentation of man's self-awareness in his relationship to even the temporal order as contributed by the medieval university? Few, if any, medieval scholars invested their time in studying the legendary question concerning the number of angels who could dance comfortably on the head of a pin. They were vastly more inclined to study such matters as the meaning of human life and the way in which it should be lived. Their study of this matter would, of course, tend to be theocentric (St. Thomas called his ethics "The Movement of the Rational Creature toward God"). If the scholar's specialty were not theology, he would probably be absorbed in early Greek and Latin thought or later Arabic thought, seeking to plumb its depths and ingest it into his own thinking and writing. Or he might be studying the stars or the elements of the earth with such instruments as were available to him. Also, as the sources reveal, he had a deep critical spirit and a very good sense of humor—a combination that seems to have become more and more rare as the centuries have passed. Perhaps its finest exemplar was a post-medieval man—a Renaissance man named Thomas More.

But with Renaissance man began the dethronement of theology
in the university. The attitudes of scholars became increasingly
homocentric; secular art and science was exalted at the expense of
the sacred. With the Reformation this course became irreversi-
ble. For now, there were at last two theologies. Even though we
realize now that in the beginning these theologies were not as far
apart as Protestants and Catholics thought they were, the fact
that they thought they were was sufficient to bring down
theology from her throne. Philosophy, without a mistress to
serve, wandered off in other directions, to become in time a
totally homocentric discipline. Secular science became master of
the university and, in a sense, of the minds of men. Sacred
science—having left the halls of the university—withdrew into
the sanctuary, where to a large extent it lost its character as
science and assumed the role of apologist and preacher. Theological learning was to be found only in the seminaries, Protestant
and Catholic, and even there suffered until quite recently from
the delusion that homiletics and apologetics were its central task
and concern.

These cursory paragraphs are not intended to exhaust an in-
exhaustible subject. They are intended to provide some context
and background for a further consideration of the relationship of
the Church and the secular university. By this time the reader
will have gathered that it is my conviction that the Church belongs
on the campus primarily in an educative and intellectual capacity.
I do not think that theology is to be forever in exile from the
university, any more than I believe that revelation is now in exile
from the world of man. For the Catholic, God's revelation is an
objective fact—the fact of God's action in history. From that
divine action have emerged certain truths, which, as indicated,
can be formulated, even if inadequately, in intellectual propositions. Those propositions are patient of meditation and study. I
do not question the fact that faith results from man's experience
with God in history—his meeting with God. I do say that this
experience is as valid as any other human experiences and is
as worthy of study precisely as a result of human experience.
Finally, I believe with the Church that theological pursuits can

unify man's knowledge and produce in him a kind of wisdom that transcends mere knowledge without ceasing to be intellectual.

Here I find myself in disagreement with Harvey Cox, who simply assumes that, although the Church has something to say to the university, she has no world-view to offer. In fact, he feels that any such thing as a world-view (theology in our sense) is an impossibility today. He is grateful, as indeed I am, that the university itself, as an institution, will never be able to provide one. What I cannot accept is that urbanized man neither needs nor wants a world-view, that he can quite happily get along without it. This proposition runs counter to all human experience, unless, as I strongly suspect, Dr. Cox includes all the "experience" that he supposes man will inevitably suffer in future eons.

I have noted that sacred science lost its traditional place in the university with the division of theology that followed the division of the churches. That is why today's ecumenical movement is so vital not only to the reunion of the churches, but also to the re-establishment of theology. Man has a way, under God's grace, of reversing the trends which, apart from grace, seem inevitable to the mind which fails to take grace into account. The philosopher of history has a difficult time in coping with this fact; the philosopher of projected history has an even more difficult time. During the nineteenth century no one could have foreseen the formation of a World Council of Churches that would succeed in bringing Protestant denominations closer to one another even to the point, in some cases, of amalgamation. As little as a decade ago it would have been impossible to predict the action taken by the Second Vatican Council in relation to the whole ecumenical movement: "The Sacred Council exhorts, therefore, all the Catholic faithful to recognize the signs of the times and to take an active and intelligent part in the work of ecumenism." (Decree on Ecumenism, I, 4)

Here, surely, is a prime challenge to the Catholic community on the secular campus. Technical discussion of theological matters must be left to the theologians, Protestant and Catholic. Ultimately it will be they who must approach the secular university with a theology formulated in such a way as to demand the consideration of faculty and administration. But there is much to be done at other levels. Since all this for the present must be extracurricular, it will call for sacrifice of time and energy on the part of faculty and students alike. Education for the coming ecumenical age will emerge in the coming decade, on the secular campus especially, as the most significant religious development of our times.

Among the "initiatives and activities" involved in a serious attempt at ecumenism the Fathers of the Council emphasize two areas of experimentation:

First, "every effort must be made to avoid expressions, judgments, and actions which do not represent the condition of our separated brethren with truth and fairness. . . ." (I, 4) This effort must be accompanied by an acknowledgment on the part of Catholics of "the truly Christian endowments from our common heritage which are to be found among our separated brethren." (*Ibid.*) Nor should it be ignored that in addition to the common heritage Catholics share with non-Catholic Christians there is also a "spiritual patrimony common to Christians and Jews" which is "so great" that the Fathers of the Council saw fit to recommend "that mutual understanding and respect which is the fruit, above all, of biblical and theological studies." (Declaration of the Relation of the Church to Non-Christian Religions, 4)

It is therefore incumbent upon the educated Catholic today to make acquaintance with genuine Protestantism and genuine Judaism, and not be content with some caricature inherited from an immature past. Prejudice cannot be set aside merely by an act of the will; it goes far too deep for that. There must be a concerted attempt to understand. Differences do exist in the doctrinal and ethical teachings of Protestants, Catholics, and Jews. Frequently, however, the real differences are not those emphasized in our folkloristic inheritance, based as it is on the emotional rather than on the intellectual. Taking all this into account, the campus Newman center of the future (I mean the near future) must be an ecumenical center. It must offer to the Catholic community the opportunity to become acquainted, through its library, its lecture series, its meetings, with representative Protestant and Jewish thought as well as the thought of the other religious traditions. The Catholic Center must be a home for dialogue on a paratheological level with faculty and students of every background. Only in this way can it prepare the educated Catholic for his role in the ecumenical movement.

Second, "Instruction in sacred theology and other branches of knowledge, especially those of a historical nature, must be presented from an ecumenical point of view, so that at every point they may more accurately correspond with the facts of the case." (II, 10) As this passage of the decree proceeds it becomes clear that this particular step in the direction of ecumenism concerns the training and education of priests and future priests. But the Council's frequent insistence upon the dignity and responsibility of the laity in the Church and in the world justifies us in applying this passage to the religious instruction of our college men and women. Even before the Council, and increasingly during and after the sessions, great ferment and excitement has come to our college campuses, where "college" theology is becoming a central issue. About two decades ago Father John Courtney Murray, S.J. (who is responsible for most of the phraseology of the Council's decree on religious liberty), writing in *Theological Studies*, proposed a theology for the layman. This was not to be a watered-down or condensed version of scientific theology, but a theology tailored to the needs and wants of the educated man and woman. He himself pioneered in the task of putting together materials for such a course. Since then he has had many collaborators and followers who have attempted to formulate a satisfactory program. Previous to that time all that was made available in Catholic colleges was a rather uninspired and uninspiring presentation of the catechetical materials which had been learned and relearned on the elementary and secondary level. No Catholic educator at the moment would pretend to be fully satisfied with the theological courses and course materials that are now in use; all are in an experimental stage and few of them have been adapted so that they fully reflect the ecumenical spirit, which for today's layman must be so vital.

The Fathers of the Council, in suggesting ways in which scientific theology may properly be adapted to ecumenical goals, also present (at least by inference) a partial program for a layman's theology:

The manner and order in which Catholic belief is expressed should in no way become an obstacle to dialogue with our brethen. It is, of course, essential that doctrine be clearly presented and in its entirety. Nothing is so foreign to the spirit of ecumenism as a false conciliatory approach which harms the purity of Catholic doctrine and obscures its assured genuine meaning.

At the same time, Catholic belief needs to be explained more profoundly and precisely, in ways and in terminology which our separated brethren too can understand. [II, 11]

The Fathers point out that "in Catholic teaching there exists an order or 'hierarchy' of truths, since they vary in their relationship to the foundation of the Christian faith." (*Ibid.*) Also, they encourage all members of the Church "while preserving unity in essentials to preserve a proper freedom . . . even in the theological elaborations of revealed truth." (I, 4) This latter instruction, as many have pointed out, reflects the spirit of the words with which Pope John XXIII opened the Council: "The deposit of faith is one thing; the way that it is presented is another. For the truths preserved in our sacred doctrine can retain the same substance and meaning under different forms of expression." (A.A.S. 54 [1962], p. 792)

Catholic men and women in the secular or Catholic college, just like Catholic priests and seminarians, need to rethink and relearn the content of their faith and its moral and ethical implications according to this program. I see it as the task of the Catholic college to produce the materials and methods necessary to implement this thinking and learning process. The work of the Newman Apostolate will be to adapt these to the lively ecumenical situation of the secular campus.

The bourgeois religion of the robot is not sufficient for these days. Often it is weakly based on misconceptions of his own religious tradition and fortified classically by a vague but prejudiced impression of other traditions. Not only does this approach (or lack of approach) to religion tend to foster religious dissension and division, but it fails to provide him with an adequate basis for any kind of genuine commitment. He gives to the propositions of faith (to the extent that he knows them) what Newman would term only "notional" assent. He accepts them simply because it is fashionable in his circle to do so; it affords him some sense of comfort without making unreasonable demands upon him. It asks only a certain external conformity, but does not enter into his motivations or in any real way affect the life he lives—a life not really distinguishable from the life of the secular man.

The radical religion of the revolutionary also falls short of the requirements of today. It is a commonplace in the Judeo-Christian tradition that God has never despaired of man, that He never will despair of man. But the radical theology of today has so far despaired of God that it has declared Him dead. It seeks to bury with Him all those traditional institutions of religion that have been responsible, under God, for the creation and preservation of the values that have contributed to the civilization of man. The values somehow are expected to remain without God and without religion as we have known it. Whether this state of things would really eventuate is at best a moot question. Previous experiments of this kind have not met with conspicuous success.

The difficulty with radical theology is that its proponents are the heirs of a succession of theologians and philosophers who regarded God as only a name and His Word as merely a human creation. It is not necessary to bury Him; it is enough to delete His name from the dictionary. When a word or a name becomes obsolete, because of its lack of meaning or relevance, it finds its proper place in histories of language and linguistics. The radical theologians have not proved that God as a Person has no relevance for modern man; they have assumed that the name *God* has no meaning for him. It is not surprising that sincere thinkers should come to such a conclusion. For there is a sense in which

God, because of His transcendence, *must* seem irrelevant to man. The Psalmist in his prayer continually sings of the incomprehensibility of God and of His ways. The Christian thinker must resort to philosophical analogies in order to speak of Him at all. Even this would be impossible were not God also immanent in His creation. Outside and apart from mystical experience man encounters God in nature and, especially, in other men. The Jew, as the result of God's action in history, encounters Him in the Law and in the Prophets. The Christian, according to his faith, meets him uniquely in Christ, the Word made Flesh. It is because of His immanence in nature and His saving action in history that we meet Him at all. And even there we touch only the fringe of His robe. But as with the sick woman in the Gospels, we believe this to be a healing touch. The name *God* means more than we can fathom.

If neither the religious robot nor the revolutionary theologian has the answer to the problem of religious commitment in our day, where does it lie? It seems to me that it lies in Newman's idea of *real* religious assent. The assent of the religious robot is merely *notional* and not *real;* the assent of the revolutionary theologian is ultimately not religious. *Real* assent is not possible without a prior understanding by the Catholic of the elements that enter into his religious tradition. Here there is required an understanding at least commensurate with his understanding of the other objects of study he pursues in the university. Anything less than this will leave him with an unbalanced view of the realities with which he must deal in his life. Further, this must be a true understanding, purged of all the infantile and adolescent elements which in most cases distort students' views of their religion and its meaning. To help the student achieve this for himself, the Newman Center must provide in the spirit of the Council the educational tools and the intellectual challenges. Yet even this process may end only with apprehension and not with assent.

Real assent is reached only when what is apprehended becomes the motivation of one's life and actions. Thus, although I believe that the educational and intellectual aspects of the work of the campus Catholic chaplain and his associates constitute the substance of their work, I recognize that the Newman Center must also provide opportunities and incentives for involvement. *Real* assent sparked by faith is a phenomenon which God by His own initiative must bring about. Nevertheless it is for us to provide the conditions and circumstances that make for a favorable response on the part of the student.

Among these conditions and circumstances, I feel that the common worship of the community takes the first place. Many of my Catholic colleagues will be disappointed that I have not spoken of liturgy as the primary and chief aspect of the work of the chaplaincy. The reason I have not done so is my conviction that the liturgy cannot establish a community: it requires a community already established. For this community already established the Eucharistic sacrifice and banquet becomes the most adequate expression of the involvement of its members—the clearest outward sign of their real assent to the demands of faith. I would agree that liturgical worship is the most important objective of the Catholic campus ministry, even though not the primary aspect of its work. It is for this reason that the campus daily Mass is of such vital importance to the Newman Apostolate everywhere. But the liturgy is much more than a means to an end; it is an end in itself. Although it includes educative elements, those elements are not the main ones. To the Mass each member of the community and the community as a whole brings the gift of a committed self—all that one is, all that one *does*, all that one *has*—to be assimilated into Christ's own gift of Himself to the Father. It is here that all the preparatory work of the Newman Center reaches its climax and finds its finest expression. The celebration must therefore be a worthy one, not so much in the external ritual and ceremony (though this is important) as in the inward dedication of all who participate. Vatican II in its sweeping liturgical reforms has opened the way to ritual usages that enable the members of the campus community to exercise their "common priesthood" in ways uniquely suited to their needs. The Mass, of course, remains the Mass as always—but now, and for the future, it will be a completely "participated" Mass in which each member of the community has his own office and place. In the campus chapel opportunities for dignified ritual experimentation are afforded in ways that remain, for the most part, difficult or impossible in the average parochial situation. In the short space of two years I have already seen and witnessed the impact of the new forms of the student Mass on our Columbia Catholic community. And I am convinced that, as time goes by, more and more students and faculty members will tend to make this Eucharistic experience the center of their day—and their lives. A liturgy such as this is already the most eloquent type of witness to the secular campus.

The *real* assent that generates in the members of the Catholic community a deep involvement in the liturgy of the Mass must also in these days motivate them to engage in a common witness of worship with all those in the academic community who, to a greater or less degree, share their beliefs. All churches recognize that ultimate unity, as well as every intermediate step, can be wrought only by God's own act, and that common prayer for unity must therefore take the first place in every program of ecumenical activity. To cite the decree on Ecumenism (II, 8):

Catholics already have a custom of uniting frequently in that prayer for the unity of the Church with which the Savior Himself, on the eve of His death, appealed so fervently to His Father: "That all may be one." [Jn. 17:21]

In certain special circumstances, such as in prayer services "for unity" and during ecumenical gatherings, it is allowable, indeed desirable, that Catholics should join in prayer with their separated brethen. Such prayers in common are certainly a very effective means of petitioning for the grace of unity, and they are a genuine expression of the ties which even now bind Catholics to their separated brethen. "For where two or three are gathered together for My Sake, there am I in the midst of them." [Mt. 18:20]

The general statement of the Council has been followed in recent weeks by the publication by the bishops of the United States of a set of guidelines for the conduct of common worship. The rules open up a wide area for experimentation regarding the form and content of such services and leave us with a challenge to our ingenuity.

The rising tide of unbelief on the secular campus has so far met only slight challenge from the forces of the combined religious bodies of students. We have concentrated so much upon our internal disagreements that we have offered no united witness to our belief. I do not deny that the differences are tragically real, or that in many instances they go very deep. But because the unitive elements are real, too, with charity and love, and in cooperation with God's grace, the differences can be ameliorated. Common worship will serve not only to create a closer unity, but also to proclaim it to the secular campus. It is imperative, therefore, that from this point on it become a significant part of the joint program of the religious bodies on campus.

There is another area in which the Newman Center must provide opportunities and incentives for those members of the academic community whose *real* assent to their religious tradition must find expression in sincere involvement—the vast area of social concern. Again, many of my Catholic colleagues (and perhaps the majority of my non-Catholic colleagues) will express disappointment that I have not given this crucial challenge to religion a more central position in this chapter. Am I closing my eyes to the peace movements and the civil rights movements that are so active on our campuses today? Am I blind to the sincere commitment of the great numbers of professors and students, often unbelievers with humanitarian rather than religious motivations? Of course not! I regard the solution of social problems as the responsibility of the Catholic as much as, if not more than, that of others. Also, with the Fathers of the Council, I see cooperation in this direction as, perhaps, the best way of building a bridge to sincere unbelievers as well as to other believers. Speaking of this matter, the Council declared:

Since in our times cooperation in social matters is very widely practiced, all men without exception are summoned to united effort. Those who believe in God have a stronger summons, but the strongest claims are laid on Christians, since they have been sealed with the name of Christ.

Cooperation among all Christians vividly expresses that bond which already unites them, and it sets in clearer relief the features of Christ the Servant. Such cooperation which has already begun in many countries, should be ever increasingly developed, particularly in regions where a social and technical revolution is taking place. It should contribute to a just appreciation of the dignity of the human person, the promotion of the blessings of peace, the application of gospel principles to social life, and the advancement of the arts and sciences in the Christian spirit. Christians should also work together in the use of every possible means to relieve the afflictions of our times, such as famine and natural disasters, illiteracy and poverty, lack of housing and the unequal distribution of wealth. (Ecumenism II, 12)

This list of the areas of social concern is obviously only suggestive, but it does include most of the problems which exercise us today in our circumstances. Furthermore, the Decree on the Apostolate of the Laity (III, 12) indicates that social responsibility is as much the business of young people as of anyone else: "Their heightened influence in society demands of them a proportionally active apostolate." Consequently, I must insist that I have no intention of minimizing the importance of the social responsibility of the Catholic campus community. In much the same way as with participation in worship, it is a necessary consequence of *real* assent. And it is the work of the Catholic chaplaincy to provide, by means of its program, the information and, by means of the liturgy, the inspiration for this type of commitment.

It does not appear to me at least that it is the duty of the chaplaincy to sponsor demonstrations and marches, or teach-ins (often hopelessly one-sided), or to be forever signing petitions. There will be occasions when such activities will be truly useful and worthwhile. Both faculty members and students should be encouraged to participate in such movements freely and according to the dictates of conscience. The opportunities to be offered by the Newman Center ought to include opportunities for service to the neighboring community. We often forget that armed conflict, looked at theologically, is only a reflection on a large scale of the lack of peace and harmony among members of families and of neighborhoods. We tend, too, to overlook the fact that no amount of civil rights talk or legislation will compensate for the effects already wrought upon a whole people by discrimination and prejudice, by all the deprivations that have brought on poverty, hopelessness and ignorance. More good can be wrought in the long run, I feel, by a program of "internship" involving committed students who give of their spare time to assist neighboring families, especially the children, to achieve a degree of self-confidence and kindle a spark of hope. The program offered by the Citizenship Council of Columbia College in cooperation with Barnard, run by and for the students, strikes me as a singularly successful effort in this direction. Already it involves hundreds of students and is having a considerable impact on the community. At Columbia the Newman Center seeks to incorporate this project as well as the projects of the neighboring churches in its program. It is hoped that this experience of internship in social concerns in college days will lead to strong commitment in adult life.

Neither the religious robot nor the radical theologian provides the answer to the problem of religious commitment in our day. The answer, I submit, is in the *real* assent of the believer to his religious tradition and his necessary and consequent involvement in liturgical and social action, all operating within an ecumenical framework. This is by no means a complete answer to the question posed earlier in this chapter: What is the theology of the Newman Apostolate; what is its philosophy? The question of the Christian's vocation as an educated man, as an intellectual, has been touched on only implicitly. The challenge that lies in the problem of marshaling all those educational and intellectual resources of the Church that are necessary to enable today's college man and woman to bring himself to the point of *real* assent has not been adequately faced. But I offer these pages as a series of observations, which, with the help of the critique of my colleagues, Catholic and non-Catholic, may help to clarify the think-ing of all of us who are engaged in the all-important task of wit-nessing to religious truth on the secular campuses of America.

I do not apologize for leaning so much as I have on the declara-tions of Vatican II. It is difficult for us to foresee what great changes will result for the Church and, therefore, for the Church's campus ministry from the working out in history and society of these constitutions and decrees. We can only project and estimate. Nor do I apologize for my frequent use of the ideas of John Henry Newman. Not only is he the patron of our work, but perhaps of all modern theologians his influence on the Coun-cil was the greatest. I should like to conclude with some hopeful words he wrote in spite of his awareness of the growing irreligion of his own time, words I borrow to make my own profession of faith:

Some persons speak of [Christianity] as if it were a thing of history, with only indirect bearings on modern times. I cannot allow that it is a mere historical religion. Certainly it has its foundations in the pres-ent. It is no dreary matter of antiquarianism; we do not contemplate it in conclusions drawn from dumb documents and dead events, but by faith exercised in ever-living objects, and by the appropriation and the use of ever-recurring gifts.

*Our communion with it is the unseen, not the obsolete.**

* *Grammar of Assent.* London, 1903, pp. 487–88.

Religious Commitment on the Campus

LYMAN T. LUNDEEN

I sat in my office at Columbia University and listened carefully to the questions the young Midwestern college student put to me. It was an easy matter to deal with his main concern—he simply wanted to know the location of the nearest church of his denomination so that his parents' insistent demands could be satisfied. They had set down as a condition of his continued study at Columbia certain minimal church-attendance requirements, and he was ready to comply just to get them out of his hair.

When he was about to leave, he turned and asked a much more difficult question. "Say," he said pointedly, "do you believe all that crap?"

Certainly, there are not many parents who insist on the kind of conditions imposed on this young man. Nor, for that matter, are there many students who would voluntarily confront a religious counselor in this manner with questions about religious belief. Yet this incident does have a wider significance, for it gives shape to the problem of religious commitment as I have seen it on the campus of a large urban university.

Here is a bright young man conversing with a minister who represents in the academic community the traditional faith. That faith, in a demanding and seemingly limiting fashion, has somehow been entangled with the last grasping controls of an older generation many miles across the country. The student is caught in the aggravation which goes with every young person's development of an adult identity. At the same time, the content of religious faith is called into question as verging on the ridiculous. Is it possible that any modern man, in a world of highly developed science and technology, could believe all those things? Surely, for a man to cling to the mysteries of faith it must require either the complete rejection of intellectual respectability or some really weird mental gymnastics. Yet the question about the faith is asked because in the university one must be concerned about

151

honesty and objectivity. Even if something doesn't make sense, an effort must be made to discover the facts. It is a kind of moral responsibility to go after the truth, even in places where you do not expect to find it.

The implications of such a brief encounter trace the broad dimensions of students' problems with religious commitment. Of course, religious commitment is only a problem for those who see it as something of value; for many students religion is no problem at all, it is only irrelevant. Still, our society and our history encourage us to see religious commitment as important and thus the relationship of the young people of our land to religious faith becomes a problem. The pressures are on in the college years to make what has been traditionally understood as religious commitment difficult, often uncomfortable, and frequently impossible during this period of development. Because of the increased impact of college and university education on our society, the nature of this pressure and its effects is of significance for all of us.

Our example provides an outline of the religious problem that is in a general way very much like that faced by students in other generations. The differences in the sixties may seem but nuances and developments of familiar themes. Yet the radical changes in the cultural situation make the same outline, the same shape, so unique that it has important implications for our understanding of our society and its future. With this in mind, let us make use of four factors in the illustration as guidelines for a look at the campus scene.

The parents' demand for church attendance focuses our attention on the traditional forms of religion, such as worship and institutional life. It also suggests an ambiguity in that tradition—religious forms are confused with parental and social authority. Religious faith has always involved some relation to structures and observances of tradition which, in coming out of the past, could readily be identified with the restrictions of a parental home or the demands of an old-fashioned society. One component of religious commitment, then, is the traditional.

In every area, practice implies theory. Traditional religious ceremony and identification with a particular religious community seems to involve intellectual commitments of one kind or another. While in any day the content of the faith would have been difficult to deal with in an academic community, in our day those problems are amplified and sharpened. The assertions of faith impinge on other areas of human experience in which knowledge is claimed on empirical grounds. Those other areas produce such useful knowledge that, by comparison, the assertions of religion seem unimportant. So the student can be expected to raise serious and penetrating questions about the claims of religion. "Do you believe all that?" is a question that in our time points to a more difficult problem than in the past. So the second aspect of religious commitment is the intellectual content that traditional faith implies.

In our example, the encounter with the student can be seen as an occasion of ethical concern. Compliance with the demands of parents or conventional society certainly involves the moral issue. In addition, the question about belief is at least partially motivated by a desire for truth, a concern for honesty, and an interest in an appropriate response to the claims of traditional faith. These ethical considerations are closely related to the concerns of religion and are therefore a third dimension of religious commitment.

The fourth relevant factor in the illustration is the involvement of a clergyman who represents a particular religious community. Such a minister is an official symbol of religious commitment and raises the question of whether a formal ministry belongs in the structure of the university. How does his particular faith and institutional identity fit in with the studied "objectivity" of academic life?

1. The Problem of Tradition

There is a powerful tendency on the part of students in the university to identify religion with tradition. Such tradition is often

seen in a monolithic way that blends the last vestige of parental
control with various conservative pressures toward conventional
morality and a social *status quo*. Religion is interpreted as a re-
pressive phenomenon and as an illegitimate justification for dealing with the radically new problems of our time according to old-
fashioned rules. Thus it is not surprising that in the context of a
sexual revolution, and in a world that vibrates with the speed of
technological change, religious commitment appears to many
students something that must be avoided at all cost. To gain their
identity as adults, and their freedom as responsible citizens of a
truly modern world, they feel they must keep themselves at some
distance from traditional religious entanglements. The tradition
that has often claimed to be a gospel of liberation looks to them
like a subtle form of limitation and bondage. Is it any wonder
that many students, when speaking of religious commitment, will
seek to express a candid and studied neutrality? As one young
Barnard student put it, without any hostility or great concern:
"When it comes to religion, I'm nothing!"

One can easily recognize the problems of students with their
tradition as something they have in common with earlier generations. Surely every young person has had to struggle with the
identification tradition brings. Or, if they haven't had a struggle,
their adoption of a traditional identity has frequently been an attempt to hide from other difficulties. Yet the response to tradition
is becoming more and more problematic. For one thing, the
world has shrunk in size so that the plurality of traditions is much
more noticeable. The fact that one has a choice among traditions
is certainly clearer than it once was. At the same time, the plurality of traditions has called their distinctiveness into question. The
result is that students are increasingly bothered by the particularity that goes with open and explicit indications of any kind of religious commitment. Religious and denominational identities are
more difficult for students to express. While they may not renounce their tradition in the sense that they will never return to
it, during their college years they are not eager to let faith carry
much weight or become overly apparent. Someday, when they

become members of a suburban church and have children of their own, things may be different, but right now they want to stay as neutral as possible in the religious realm. One can note with interest or concern that since the period of education in university centers is lengthening, one difference in the contemporary situation is that the period of neutrality tends to become a permanent stance rather than a stage on the way to commitment.)

The tendency to shy away from open religious commitment affects even those students with a strong and fairly positive religious background. Students who ten years ago would have been active members of student Christian organizations or other religious groups, and who would have rejoiced in their religious identity, adopt a very different attitude today. While they are interested in service and concerned about moral issues, the identification with a particular religious point of view is largely avoided. An example of this can be seen in many of the students who now work in our coffee house. When the Chaplain of Columbia was quoted in *Time* magazine as having said that the Postcrypt was not a "Christian coffee house," most of the students who operate the establishment openly rejoiced. One can see their identification with this proclamation as a declaration of independence from a religious tradition.

At the same time, careful reading of the religious-preference cards at Columbia and Barnard reveals an increasing appreciation for religious neutrality. The percentage of students who are willing to express a religious preference decreases a little each year, and for many, a blank card is not enough to indicate their lack of specific religious interest. A good number will take the extra time and effort to write in such comments as "I don't believe anything" or "I have absolutely no religious preference." Even for those who do express a preference, in many instances it is like a last tip of the hat to an old acquaintance.

One is never quite sure whether the resistance to religious identification stems from real concern to appreciate all traditions or from the recognition that none of them really counts when it comes to their peculiarities. It would appear that for many stu-

dents the principle of tolerance has been elevated to such a degree
that it really becomes the rejection of all religious faith as relevant and decisive. "All religions are valid for those who follow
their teachings" quite easily becomes "But no religion is valid for
me," and the combination of the two assertions amounts to the
denial of all real validity in any religion. This is an intellectual
formulation of a sincerity criterion. "It doesn't matter what you
believe as long as you are sincere." What matters is sincerity, not
the particular beliefs, and what is needed then is not tolerance but
some adequate test of sincerity.

Of the pressures that make religious identification difficult,
perhaps none is more significant than the tendency toward
polarization between conservative and liberal positions in the sixties. A dichotomy has been established in which one seems to
have to choose between the past and the future. Appreciation of
the resources of the past and the patterns that have proved themselves in experience is set over against an openness to the radical,
changing world that demands unique solutions. Tradition is seen
as opposed to change in a world that moves so quickly and drastically that there doesn't seem to be any real option but to reject
tradition for the sake of the future. This kind of polarization of
views has not occurred in the past in the same way, when the rate
of change was slower. Tradition was seen as an opportunity for
selection, rather than as a simple matter of acceptance or rejection. Yet this radical option is precisely what the students of the
sixties face, an apparent choice between identification with tradition and the creative acceptance of the future with its novelty. It
is surely not surprising that the future is the more attractive of
these two alternatives.

Unfortunately, such a drastic choice is a deceptive and unpro-
ductive prospect. It is generally the misuse of tradition and the
distortion of traditional resources that have led to such an option
—in other words, the older generation will have to take much of
the blame for this kind of problem in the lives of our young people. First, we have misused the traditional elements in our experience to forestall a recognition of the changing world and to hide

from our responsibilities. In the sixties this kind of hypocrisy on the part of those who have transmitted the tradition is clearer than it has been in the past. The future is upon us in such a shocking way that the manner in which tradition has been made an excuse for perpetuating the *status quo* is open for all to see. Second, the tradition itself has been distorted to justify social conditions and our own failure to deal with human problems. This has happened not only because of perversity, but as a result of apathy and neglect. Whatever the reason, the best of the religious tradition often has not been transmitted at all. The distorted tradition cannot be seen by young people as a resource for solving today's problems. Rather, it seems necessary to reject the entire tradition in order to be able to get to the tasks at hand.

Hypocrisy is nothing new in the annals of religion. It happens that the hypocrisy of the older generation stands out in our time with a clarity that it formerly did not have. The civil rights movement is the foremost instance of the way the younger generation's sensitivity to the demands of brotherhood and justice has called into question the commitments and the traditions of their parents. Today's students have suddenly become aware of the ways in which their elders have used traditional religion to shore up conventional morality and social controls. Religious commitments have been instrumental in controlling youth and keeping them within the limits of conventional behaviour. Parents have made religion a sanctimonious enhancement of their own authority, and they have frequently coupled it with blatant hypocrisy on their own part. Children have been taught more by their parents' behaviour than by their words. What they have learned—and it comes out clearly on the college level—is that religion is for controlling the kids and for keeping the social structure stable. Adults don't have to take its demands too seriously, as long as they know enough not to rock the boat in which the young of necessity must ride. If the boat needs rocking, throw the religious tradition over first and change will come more easily. The hypocrisy of parents who see to it that their children are taught a religion that they themselves put little stock in makes the rejection of traditional religion even easier for the college student. Indeed, it formulates the option so as to make the rejection of tradition almost necessary on moral grounds.

The misuse of tradition has led to the opinion that religious commitments limit our flexibility in the technological world rather than free us for action. Looking back historically, our young people can see the ineffectiveness of the Hebrew-Christian tradition in dealing with problems of war, class injustice, and scientific advancement. Where components of the tradition would have challenged the *status quo*, they have been neglected or interpreted in such a way as to maintain peace in the churches and a neat separation between the ideal of love and its exemplification in social structures. Because of this, many religious people are surprised to discover that Jeremiah and Paul spent so much of their time in jail! And the early church promoted a brand of communism and shared jointly the ownership of property.

If the traditional religious commitments are to have something to offer to our college students, it must be on the basis of a return to tradition as an opportunity for selection. An example of this kind of an appeal to tradition is given by the noted theologian and martyr, Dietrich Bonhoeffer. Bonhoeffer was put to death by the Nazi regime just as that diabolical machine was on the point of collapse. Among other cryptic comments set down during his last days in prison, he suggested that we were approaching the time of no religion at all. Many have seized upon his view as a justification for the simple rejection of traditional religious points of view. It seems to others that what Bonhoeffer was calling for was a re-evaluation of the religious tradition and the recognition that some kinds of religious faith could be abolished with no regrets whatsoever. He rejoiced in the demise of what he called "religion" because he saw it as a perversion of the Christian faith. Christianity was focused in the incarnation of God in Christ which eternally bound man and God together, and by implication required a faith which would keep the sacred and the secular in an intimate and creative relationship. Bonhoeffer saw the religious mentality as perverting that faith and separating the sacred and secular into mutually exclusive compartments. He therefore called for a selection of the relevant and liberating faith from the traditional distortions that had emasculated it. He asserted the necessity of taking from tradition that which retained an authentic and liberating validity for our time, and rejecting that which was limiting and anachronistic. Bonhoeffer suggests an attitude toward traditional religion that is selective rather than a radical choice between acceptance and rejection.

In a similar way, it is up to the religious institutions of our land to seek radical reform of their own use of tradition if the problem of confronting students is to be changed. The misuse of tradition and the dogmatic distortion of the liberating elements of the faith must be recognized and avoided. Essentially, this is a problem of translation. Where the traditional faith is claimed as liberating, then that freedom must be translated into a joyous flexibility in the face of modern problems. Worship and institutional identity must be transformed so that their relevance for secular and human concerns is clarified. Priorities must be set forth so that an honest evaluation of traditional faith is possible. Such efforts will not mean that students will throng to the churches, or that they will rejoice in their traditions, but it will mean that if they reject the faith they will do so on better grounds than now seems to be the case. Certainly, not all of the difficulty with tradition is due to parental or institutional distortions. But there is enough of that ingredient to make it crucial for us to insure that our young people are aware of the alternatives involved in tradition itself.

This is the challenge that faces the religious communities of our land. It includes the recognition that the problems students have in identifying with traditional religion are to a large degree the making of the older generation. At the same time, it involves seeing these problems in relation to the rapid changes in social and political options that have been brought about by technological change. The novelty of our situation demands an adventurous spirit and a faith formulated to support such an attitude. New answers are required if we are not to blow this old world of ours

sky-high. We cannot afford simply to mouth the old solutions
that have only the support of age. We need the courage to launch
out on new patterns of problem-solving; if our religious traditions do not provide help in this matter, what can our young people do but reject them? If there are resources in the Western religious tradition that will encourage productive solutions to the
problems of humanity, then someone had better start making
those resources clear. Student apathy of the fifties has given way
to involvement and action. Now they are aroused to look for answers, they are motivated to get busy making this world a more
human place to be. Therefore, their problems with tradition
ought to be a reforming force on the tradition itself. We must at
least recognize where as parents and as a society we have undercut authentic Hebrew-Christian tradition by forming it in our
own image and to our own liking. We can also see that the student reaction to tradition and its resources could be as frightening in its extremes as their elders' distortion of the tradition. It is
then crucial that something be done to open doors for both
groups toward an honest and creative recovery of what is vital in
our religious heritage.

2. *Intellectual Problems*

The intellectual content of the faith has increasingly been rele-
gated to the periphery of academic concern. As scientific development and technological achievement have moved with dazzling
rapidity to bring about the knowledge explosion, they have
brought in their wake a pervasive skepticism about the importance of fundamental religious assertions. The assertions in question are those that claim to express knowledge beyond the competence of science. Where just a few years ago the relation of
religious knowledge and scientific knowledge was a significant
subject for discussion, to a large degree the discussion itself has
now become irrelevant. It is not so much that theological assertions meet a direct challenge from some secular point of view; it
is almost assumed that there is really no significant issue to argue

about. The old concern with the truth of religious assertions gave way to questions about the meaning of religious language. Now even that concern seems largely to be ignored.

The problem with religious commitment for the student often focuses on the nature of these assertions of faith. The student is faced with accepting as a part of his religious commitment numerous claims about the nature of reality, the meaning of life, and a whole collection of semihistorical accounts of miracles, mythology, and supernatural revelations. Given the mood of the academic community, these beliefs are readily labeled "religious", but at the same time they are surrounded by a skepticism that makes them both unbelieveable and irrelevant.

Some representatives of traditional religious belief have tried to show that these intellectual claims of religion are not essential to faith itself. They have attempted to make the faith relevant and safe from scientific criticism by stressing its existential aspects. The assertions of the faith are not so much about God and the supernatural as they are expressions of a style of life and a description of a human attitude. The response of faith becomes a matter of subjective stance, and the intellectual claims of the tradition are classified as a kind of outmoded metaphysics and mythology. In this context, contemporary secular points of view are challenged not on the basis of the esoteric knowledge of revelation, but by appealing to an openness to the future. The current interest in the "death of God" among theologians and others is an example of this kind of approach carried to its natural result. The emphasis is on subjective human behavior rather than on claims about objective and ultimate truth. The result of this kind of theology, in combination with the contemporary academic mood, has been that powerful support is given to the notion that the intellectual claims of religion simply don't count. In many circles, there has been a kind of spontaneous agreement between church and world that theology is dispensable. Who needs it? As one denominational executive said recently, "On the university level theological distinctions really don't make any difference!"

The student who is confronted with religious claims is not

quite sure what they involve. Do I have to believe in God or
don't I? Should I worry about miracles like the Resurrection?
Does the Bible carry the authority of Divine revelation? Such
questions are underlined by a mild acquaintance with Biblical
criticism and the "new" theologies. On the one hand, it appears
to the student that religious faith does entail very peculiar "faith"
assertions that move well beyond the realm of empirical verifica-
tion; he is ready to raise serious questions about them. But, on the
other hand, he finds people within the religious community itself
who seem to hold to the faith while letting these assertions dimin-
ish in importance and even finally disappear. His problem, then,
becomes the justification of religious faith as distinctive and
worthwhile. The student is not prepared to accept the traditional
intellectual content of the faith, but at the same time it is hard for
him to see what religion has to offer if this content is excluded. In
both cases the relation of faith to assertions about ultimate reality
is the issue. The pressure is on the student to reject those assertions and to let traditional religious faith go along with them.

 Of course, there are actually many different reasons why the
acceptance of an intellectual content in religion presents a problem. On the campus they are developed and focused to such a degree that even to claim the importance of such content can be
very uncomfortable. One of the strongest factors here has been
the phenomenal success of modern science. Concentration on science and its methods has fostered in the academic community a
pervasive skepticism as to the nature of ultimate reality and a persistent relativism as to values. The pragmatic achievement of science has made its claims to knowledge normative and tended to
separate facts from values. As science is the realm of reason and
allows us to make useful descriptions of experience that we call
knowledge, so there is a personal realm of values where preference is largely emotional, private, and separated from the objective and rational. Objectivity is the key to scientific achievement,
and that key is shaped by eliminating as far as possible all reference to value. The success of this studied objectivity has pushed
discussion of values into the background. Values, however, must

be dealt with and the mood of the campus is such as to make them strictly subjective on the one hand and to assert them very dogmatically on the other. Like all relativism, the explicit tolerance of the campus is not always so open to other points of view. In conversation one can hear the relativist objection raised against religious faith, for instance. One student said to me recently, "I don't object to your faith, but I do object to any suggestion that it might be good for anyone else." As long as another person is relativistic at the same points, the campus relativist is happy, but he is not so self-critical as to see the way in which his own position makes dogmatic claims on others.

The inherent contradiction in campus relativism becomes visible when a heated issue arises in the context of emotion and argument. Relativism works until someone comes along and feels it necessary to appeal to the "moral issue" as a means of either opposing or supporting a cause like the war effort in Vietnam. Then the subjectivity of values disappears and the "right" conclusion is supposed to be immediate and obvious. An ambiguity like this suggests that the separation of facts and values is no long-range solution.

The explicit relativism in the area of religious claims and values is of first importance here, because this is the pressure the student who is dealing with the question of religious commitment feels. He is not generally in a position to criticize the presuppositions of his peers. The student's conclusion, often unspoken out of deference to those who might still count belief about the supernatural important, is that differences in religious assertions about God or the meaning of life can be reduced to the attitudes and feelings of a particular individual. They can be explained by their sociological and psychological origins and while they say something about our communities and ourselves, they say nothing about objective reality and give us no clue to the broad meaning of life. They are thus important for the person who holds them, but surely they are nothing to argue about nor a significant focus for academic concern. Even the growth of religion departments in our universities can be seen as an expression of this attitude toward religious faith. Religion becomes an interesting academic discipline because it enables us to discover why people should have once thought that differences in religious belief were important. The study of artifacts and legends takes the place of the practice of religion as a viable option in the modern world.

The mood that puts pressure on students to discount religious assertions is both relativistic and positivistic. It settles for radical disagreement in areas of value and commitment by placing these aspects of human experience in a compartment beyond the competence of reason. It is assumed that what is valid for one person in these areas is of no vital relevance to anyone else. The mood is positivistic in the sense in which all positivism settles for certain irreducible brute facts and declines to seek understanding that might explain those facts. The brute facts in this instance are those that are amenable to scientific method, and they exclude as much as possible all reference to value, metaphysics, and religion. Such relativism and positivism is in effect the narrowing of experience to its internal dimensions. It excludes the notion of transcendence and puts concern with the reality that makes our experience possible beyond human access. Metaphysics and theology are pretty much in the same boat, in that both seek to refer to the very structure of reality and the meaning of our total experience. It is just this movement toward ultimate reality that is difficult in the academic community. God and revelation are seen as old-fashioned ways of shrouding the limits of man's experience and knowledge. They were used to cover the gaps that tended to be frightening because of the unknown elements involved. Metaphysics was a similar endeavor that attempted to understand and evaluate the whole of reality on the basis of the little already known. Now, in a scientific age, in Bonhoeffer's terms, in "a world come of age," man is supposedly mature enough to live with a clear recognition of the gaps in his knowledge and with the acceptance of the necessary limitations of his capabilities without the supports of God and metaphysics.

The point is that one does not have to work at attaining this point of view on the campus—it is in the very air we breathe. It is a mood; it is not the clear conviction of all concerned, but a steady pressure in common contacts which surrounds the discussion of almost any subject imaginable. It puts persuasive force on the student to move with it and to find battles to be fought within its context rather than against it. It carries with it the weight and power of the last fifty years of scientific achievement and the sudden shrinking of our world to a highly technological society where cultures and nations blend into a universal civilization. In that world-wide society with its technological agreement, religious beliefs about the nature and will of God are not the basis for argument or discussion. No one is denied the right to believe, but he is only required not to think his beliefs of any ultimate importance for others. One is free to follow any religion at all as long as it is recognized that no religious distinctions make any vital difference.

This being the mood of the campus, those who are seriously concerned about the place of religion can take one of two steps. They can accept the premises of the campus mood and try to show that religious commitment is important in ways that do not impinge on the realm of knowledge or science. They then run no risk of doing battle with science for the field of knowledge, but they are in danger of making religion superfluous. Or they can contend that the current mood of the student community does not reflect the last word in matters of knowledge and truth.

The latter choice I would see as the more promising option, and it is an alternative that can muster some support in the academic community. That support comes from three sources:

First there are those scientists who find the complexities of experience too far-reaching to allow narrow theories of interpretation. They are not prepared to let a dogmatic approach to the limits of science preclude possibilities of knowledge in areas that would expand the system. They see the intimate relation of value and fact in the scientific process itself and they are prepared to consider how faith and knowledge are related. With these scientifically oriented scholars stand some professional philosophers who have moved beyond the brand of linguistic philosophy that outlawed metaphysics and defined the separation of values from facts. These philosophers are interested in metaphysics once again and are willing to see the relationships of speculative commitments to the entire structure of inquiry.

There is a second source of support that is rooted in the religious tradition and attempts to restate the problem of faith and reason. Teilhard de Chardin is a Roman Catholic example of this movement. As a priest and a paleontologist he attempted to put Christianity and science together in a unified structure, and his work has drawn the interest of both theologians and scientists. Efforts in a similar direction can be seen on the Protestant side. John Cobb's book, *A Christian Natural Theology*, exemplifies a number of attempts to show how religious claims are related to other claims about reality. This task is certainly far from completed, but at least some scholars have resumed work on this old problem.

A third source of support for the recovery of a creative relationship between faith and knowledge can be seen in the urgency with which technological development demands critical and decisive control of its application. For many in the technological fields, it is becoming clear that we can make any kind of world we want but that direction is lacking to give guidance and purpose to our creation. Suddenly the very objectivity of science becomes a threat because it is not sensitive to the values of the human community in which it has been developed. Out of this comes a demand for some clear directive as to the kind of society that is truly human, and we find ourselves in a position where a commitment to values in the context of knowledge is essential. This, it seems to me, is precisely the religious question, for to address ourselves to the priority of values is to approach specific suggestions which when developed take the form of religious commitment.

In the very irrelevance of religious assertions, then, there is an issue in the secular community that may point to a vital need for the recovery of intellectually respectable content in religious faith. The attention of the university community is focused upon those areas wherein productive and useful knowledge can be attained. This has meant a primary concern for science and the universal tools it provides for dealing with experience. Even in the social sciences, statistics and quantified data rule the field and the concerns that cannot be handled mathematically and scientifically become less and less significant. Still, in the same academic context in which the facts of science are exalted, there is an intense concern for human values and social justice. Indeed, fusing the realities of technological progress with a concern for a humanized society is the central problem of our time. It is this relationship of fact and value that is problematic and it is in just this area that the content of religious faith used to fall. In this sense, the problem of intellectual content in religious faith has a direct relevance to a crucial secular concern, even though this importance is not generally recognized on the academic scene.

It can be granted that none of these challenges to the prevailing mood of the campus demands the adoption of a particular religious point of view or a traditional set of values. What they do demand is the consideration of questions of values and the critical application of those values to science and technology. They demand that we deal with the religious question and answer it in a manner more positive and direct than the popular attempt to brush it aside as an irrelevant and meaningless concern. They demand that we take seriously the possibility of a kind of knowledge in the religious realm.

This sets the task for the religious institutions and leaders in the academic community. For the sake of our students, and for the sake of our society, it is essential that we once again tackle the problem of faith and reason. The easy appeal to Thomas Aquinas and the Middle Ages will not do. Nor will the ready separation of faith from reason that has developed in Protestantism work any longer. We must instead explore all the alternatives between these two solutions and discover some way of putting knowledge and faith together again in such a fashion that both facts and values will be taken seriously and reconciled to contribute the balance and harmony required for a creative and truly human society.

The message that must be carried to the students of this generation is that a positivistic and relativistic approach to religious claims is not the only alternative. There are other options for man in the twentieth century. Indeed, it would appear that if man is to survive as man, he will have to pick another option. Perhaps God is not dead, but only being held for ransom by the current mood, and religious commitment will once again become relevant when we have been willing to pay the price of re-examining our basic suppositions both in science and religion.

3. The Ethical Dimension

The problem of religious commitment on the campus is reflected in a striking manner by the ethical dimension. Religious commitment has always involved the concern for doing the right thing, a serious and persistent interest in the most appropriate response to man's environment both in its total scope and in its details. Generally, a code of morality or at least guidelines for a way of life have gone along with allegiance to a particular religious point of view. Such concern for an honest and appropriate response to the human situation is clearly present on the campus, even though it is apt to express itself outside explicit identification with religious tradition and theology. Indeed, it is at this point that one can see the student generation come closest to the best of the Hebrew-Christian tradition.

The distortion of that tradition or the failure to understand its basic thrust tends to make the student hesitant to identify his concern with that tradition or, in many instances, even seeing the parallel concern of great religious figures. Nevertheless, the demand for honesty on the campus and the interest in human values expressed there sets this generation of students apart as reflecting the ethical component of religious commitment with great intensity. Their ethical concern may be riddled with difficulties when it comes to articulating positive solutions to human problems. Or, while it may very well be blind to the importance of structural and institutional continuities, it is a powerful and persuasive challenge for modern man to find the most appropriate way of dealing with the realities of technological culture and the needs of human beings.

This kind of concern should be recognized as a legitimate and essential part of our religious heritage. The motivation behind it and the courage with which it is sometimes expressed deserve the serious appreciation of our religious institutions and their leaders.

Evidence of the current high degree of ethical concern is not only found in the honesty that leads young students to challenge religious traditions on moral and intellectual grounds, it is also found in their willingness to become involved in action intended to make society a fairer and more human structure. Students can be aroused these days to social action in which they are willing to give of their time and effort even when their involvement includes personal risk and considerable sacrifice. This does not mean only that so-called radicals with obvious signs of nonconformity are willing to take to the streets in protest, but that moderate, well-dressed, clean-shaven, and studious types will also take time for projects of social reform demanding a great deal of solid commitment. The willingness of students who could well content themselves with competitive academic achievements or with their own personal pleasure to volunteer their services in tutoring underprivileged children and other efforts to change the complexion of society for the better is both amazing and encouraging. Certainly there are those who are apathetic about social issues, or too wrapped up in their own concerns for success to worry about anything else, but the over-all picture presents something quite different from the apathy described in the fifties.

The novelty is that in the ethical dimension, the pressure is on for the student to involve himself with others in doing the right thing. Involvement, surrounded by ethical concern, is the order of the day in the same context in which traditional religion and its creeds are forced to the periphery of interest. Where in terms of the formal, traditional expressions of religion and in relation to the assertions of faith the pressure is against religious commitment, in the realm of the ethical the pressure swings to the other side. That pressure has been so great that the students are exercising a prophetic function for the society and for the religious institutions themselves. Their basically secular attempts to act responsibly need to be seen in relation to religious faith, and as having clear and healthy effects on the religious communities of our land. When the students dare to get involved and lay their future on the line in the name of honesty and morality, suddenly the churches remember what the liberating message was all about. Abruptly, the possibility for reform in religious traditions becomes a live option.

Ethical concern without adherence to cult or creed may not be the fullness of religious commitment, but it is certainly a vital corrective in the contemporary situation. At this particular stage in our nation's life and at this crucial level of technological development, an intense ethical concern is required for humanity to find the forms in which man can prosper both as an individual and in community. The students' involvement and concern, at this point, provides a much-needed wedge in the cultural marriage of religion and the *status quo* that could well lead to the creative liberation of a dynamic and renewed religious faith. Such a faith would be open to the changes and adventure of the future, and would be a resource for a society that uses technological achievement to serve the vital interests of humanity.

While one can rejoice in the hope and the courage of the students' ethical concern, it is also necessary to recognize that problems exist. Here the problem with religious commitment is not in an attitude of rejection but in the intensity of commitment to one aspect of religious concern in separation from factors that seem to offer complementary strengths. In the context of our discussion, this means the espousal of ethical concern apart from the perspective of tradition and without the explicit articulation and criticism of the intellectual content of commitment.

The ethical concern of students raises problems because it tends to be without the positive direction required for concrete solutions to social problems. Having cut themselves off from the traditional religious institutions and effectively called attention to the negative aspects of the tradition, they have also lost the creative and liberating side of human experience that was collected in the tradition. Without the perspective of distance that tradition could give, the students point out what is wrong with society and call attention to injustice and immorality, but their judgment of possible solutions seems limited. They can call for honesty and for humanity so that their voice is heard and the impact of their criticism is forceful. Yet, should someone ask what structures are required for a just society or upon what understanding of human nature we should build the new society, they are at a loss to give positive suggestions. Criticism they can provide, but constructive solutions are not so evident.

Even some of the criticism itself is tainted by an ambiguity rooted in the rejection of tradition in such a wholehearted fashion. The students end up appealing to aspects of the tradition in a subtle way that they would avoid at all costs if such an appeal were more obvious. Consider the fashion in which some of their criticisms imply a clarity in matters of morality that is almost puritanical. Right and wrong are seen as black and white, and their appeal for honesty and justice can become so rigorous as to cut down any attempts at partial achievement or solutions by compromise. Among the left wing, this leads to a complete antagonism toward institutions and social structures as they exist, combined with the harshest judgments upon those who happen to be in power. Within the right wing, concern that claims ethical motivation leads to puritanical judgments against those who would change the structure and a strange optimism about those on the top of the heap. The ambiguity in both cases is that moral judgments applied to the current scene tend to hide their potent presuppositions from criticism and yet they are applied as though good and evil were as easily discerned as black and white.

An appreciation of our religious traditions would at the very least show this kind of ethical precision for what it is, a modern form of puritanism. If it were seen in this perspective, our students would be less apt to pick this approach to moral judgment. In other words, because our students are sensitive to moral issues but without the perspective of an appreciation of the religious tradition, they are capable of being misled by the clarity of certain issues. The fact that segregation is so clearly evil in its moral dimension can lead them to believe that all the crucial issues of the day are equally obvious. This of course precludes the necessary consideration of alternative points of view and can make of ethical concern a source of arrogance and intolerance. Intense ethical concern—sincerity if you will—can prohibit the discovery of adequate but imperfect solutions to the complex problems that humanity must face. It can discourage those who seek to deal honestly and realistically with difficult community issues and in this way lead to chaos and cruelty rather than the explicit goals it proclaims.

In this same direction the protests of the students, even though they are fundamentally rooted in ethical concern, can develop into blind and dangerous ends in themselves. Without the students' being aware of the fact, the content of the protest can become a means for dealing with personal problems rather than an instrument for changing society. To my mind, there is no question but that some of the passion that passes in the academic community for ethical concern has slipped over into a powerful subconscious desire on the part of students to dissociate themselves from the guilt of the social structures in which they have to participate. This switch in purpose leads to an inability to keep the tactics of protest related to their expressed goals. In the students' eagerness to express their displeasure with society in regard to the war in Vietnam, or in relation to social justice, they can become naïve and almost oblivious to the results of their tactics. Even granting the folly of others who take no action because they cannot find perfect tactics, it is no solution to allow the tactics themselves to become the goal. For instance, when some columnists questioned the advisability of certain protests against the war in Vietnam on the grounds that they might bring about results exactly the opposite of those intended, some students had obvious difficulty in recognizing the tactical nature of the discussion. It almost seemed that to challenge their tactics was to challenge their purpose, even though the columnists had established themselves publicly as supporting the purposes of the demonstrations. This is a real danger with the highest kind of ethical concern. We can become so wrapped up in our own protest that the expression of our ethical concern in a critical and self-justifying fashion becomes an end in itself.

It is in the discussion of ends and methods of achieving them that the rejection of the intellectual content of religion becomes a problem. In this area one cannot avoid talking about the nature of man even if one has given up on the possibility and importance of discussing the nature of God. The effectiveness of direct action and public protest is directly related to the kind of response that can be expected from human beings. At the same time, the kind of society that is possible is dependent on the amount of optimism we can realistically have in regard to man and institutions. The ethical and moral concerns of students imply assertions about man and his nature, but such assertions are not usually explicit, nor are they subject to criticism and comparison with other alternatives. One of the reasons for this is the rejection of the kind of intellectual content that includes theology. It is not seen that all that talk about God was relevant to human needs precisely because of what it implied about man. Can individuals be trusted to do the right thing without the controls of law? Many students imply that this is the case, and they do it often by selecting a group of people that can be trusted over against a group that cannot. Conservatives are hesitant to trust the poor, but they have their doubts about the wealthy and the powerful. Or, if they are liberal enough, like the New Left, they trust everybody and contend that it is the structures that have made men behave badly. All of this I would see as belonging to a level of inquiry close to the discussions of theological content that have taken place within our religious tradition, and I do not believe that we shall see really constructive solutions to social problems until we take seriously our need to discuss on this level and to exercise the greatest possible creative and critical use of our reason on these issues. Some have said about contemporary claims of the death of God that they really point to the death of Man. The rejection of theological content as a decisive and important element in man's collective experience has meant just that—the loss of productive discourse about the nature and meaning of Man.

In this fashion student ethical concern can have a negative impact unless its direction is turned toward a kind of theological reflection. Like all demands for radical honesty, this one too can lead not to a solid and positive stand but to an extreme skepticism the foundation of which is absolutely nothing but sand. Honesty must be balanced with the faith that allows us to put our weight on partially verified conclusions. Demands for moral integrity must be qualified by a willingness to solve some problems tomorrow and a flexibility that allows tentative and hesitant steps on the road to perfection. Extreme demands for honesty and integrity can become as self-defeating as blatant hypocrisy and compromise. Honesty, pushed to its limits, condemns all institutions and all men. The black-and-white moral judgments of an aroused student generation can result in the same blanket condemnation. If it works on those who disagree with us, it can be turned to work on us too.

These inconsistencies in the students' espousal of ethical concerns do not discredit the validity of the causes they uphold. They point to a task that faces our society in putting our religious heritage together again in a context in which reason and faith can function in a complementary way without the emasculation of either. With this task in mind, the students' involvement in the social issues of the day becomes a challenge to church and society to take up the task before it is too late. The shoe has been put on our foot, so to speak. We must wear it. The ethical sensitivity of the college student is not a threat to the structures or to sacred institutions. It is not a denial of religious commitment for the sake of revolution. It is a challenge—a cry—for assistance and cooperation in a world in which revolution is a concrete fact and

faith of any vital kind must deal with facts creatively and
responsibly.

4. The Function of a Religious Ministry

A religious ministry on a secular campus is one reflection of the
concern of religious communities for the issues and the persons in
the university. It is the formal sign of the interaction and inter-
penetration of the community of worship and the community of
learning. The one group finds its identity in an explicit claim
about the relation of sacred and secular; the other exalts the
secular as its primary concern and treats the sacred only where it
is necessary to do so as history and scholarship reveal man's cultic
and theological preoccupation. The one community is made up
of people who acknowledge the presence and power of God and
who claim that human experience is truncated without the transcendent dimension. The other community is an institution for
learning that has earned the right to autonomy in its own realm
of competence, and that tends to limit serious inquiry and discussion to areas where reason can work independent of faith. The
religious community names God as an additional demand and resource in the human quest. The university sets its hand to solving
man's problems with essentially human resources, available and
functional without reference to any transcendent realm.

These communities and their diverse interests are interrelated
without the necessity of a formal institutional ministry. Members
of churches and synagogues are also committed and respected
members of the university. Whatever ministry the religious institutions have must recognize that faith is already present on the
campus in many ways. Teachers, administrators, and students
fulfill a ministry by their presence on the scene. Nevertheless,
there are functions that can justify the more formal presence of
the religious institutions in the structure and life of the university.

The formal religious ministry on the campus represents a
perspective not necessarily the concern of the university by it-

self. The ministry expresses the peculiar combination of tradition, theology, and ethics characteristic of the religious point of view. The university's recognition of this perspective follows from its need to explore all the alternatives, and from the vivid apprehension that multiple options and resources will be required to resolve educational and cultural problems in a humane and moral manner. It is the claim of almost any religious perspective that questions about morality and the priority of values can best be asked in a context where an appreciation of religious traditions and a critical understanding of faith assertions are combined with a developed ethical concern. Thus, in the broadest sense, religious faith makes claims for itself as a resource in the academic process. The university, aware that all the answers are not yet in, may be well advised to accept and encourage a multiplicity of perspectives where the religious dimension is in dialogue and persuasive encounter with all the rest. And in that encounter, the wider the spectrum of specific faiths, the more creative and constructive will be the educational result. Faith, even specific faiths, is not something to fear in a free educational system unless hidden and beyond explicit criticism. By recognizing the relevance of the religious perspective, the university may even allow more honest evaluations of other points of view as their faith components are brought out.

Representing the religious community and its traditions, the campus ministry presents the claim that judgments of a theological nature are relevant to human concerns. At the very least, it insists that the kinds of question that have been dealt with in theological discussion are crucial for the decisions about direction and values man is now being forced to make. If one is unwilling to see the significance of theology in reference to God, attention should be brought to questions about man that are theological in the sense that they ask about the priority of values. "Is there anything more valuable than everything else?" is a question of this type and, while it can be understood as a theological inquiry, it also has direct relevance for the direction and shape of human society. "How far, and under what circumstances, can men be trusted?" is another question that impinges on the same area. If the nature of man in terms of his capacity for creation and destruction, for love and for hate, is crucial in the development of a structure for technological society or a solution to the political confrontation between communism and the "free" world, then it is of decisive importance that it be discussed in the academic communities and that answers to this kind of question in theological contexts be taken into consideration.

In this sense, the presence on campus of formal religious ministries provides a check on narrow theories of experience. They are surely not the only barrier to dogmatic theories, but they can give some balance in this regard. One can call it a little bit of irrationality added to the efficiency of the structure, if you will, but in the long run it may lead instead to broader and wider conceptions of reason and knowledge. Theology may also let in wishful thinking and illusion, but the risk must be run in view of the problems and potential that are at our fingertips. Science and society are pressing now on the very boundaries of experience. On those boundaries they are being forced to make decisions that affect everyone as they choose the goals and directions of human development. What is needed as those choices are made is a broad spectrum of alternatives in which ideas and models are plentiful. Theological assertions have attempted to deal with the issues of that boundary situation where fact and value meet, and it would seem worthwhile to be hesitant and careful about discounting their value in the present situation. But even granting that a religious ministry appears irrational, it may well be that this is precisely one of the needs of the university. When IBM cards carry the day, and students and faculty cannot stop the machine without their own destruction, then a degree of irrationality should be welcome. A perspective beyond efficiency and achievement seems of real value on the contemporary university scene, and if religious ministries provide this for students, faculty, and administration their presence has some justification.

The religious perspective, at its best, is one of broad concern and mediation. Recognizing the complexity of human change and the ambiguity of motivation in all of us, this point of view provides a concern for persons and the patterns of change well beyond the demand for performance and competition that can so easily dominate the academic institutions of a technological culture. This means concern for the successful and the dropouts, the apathetic and the "walking wounded." It means mediation among administration, faculty, and students and open-ended interest in every sector of the university.

If religious ministries provide this kind of support to the persons in the academic process, it is to be expected that administrators and others responsible for the total impact of the universities will be happy to have them around to assist in keeping the process of learning and teaching sensitive to persons and their values.

A second function of the formal ministry is a kind of representative participation in the university on behalf of the religious communities of the land. These communities are frequently large and they have a great deal at stake in what happens in the universities. This is especially true now that the university has become the central path for success and a dominant influence on the shape of society. While the religious communities certainly have no right to control the direction education takes, they do have a right and even a responsibility to be involved in the fundamental choices that will determine the patterns and values of the future society. As students want participation in the decisions that affect their destiny, so the religious communities of our land ought to be parties in the great academic endeavor. Surely this means that they will have to come willing to participate honestly and without coercion, but on those terms one can see why the university may even welcome them to the cooperative effort. The crises and opportunities society now faces are so great in both threat and promise that every resource of man must be brought to bear on human problems. There are leaders in the university who see the religious communities as potential resources in this area, and they do not have to be persuaded of the importance of the formal presence of a religious ministry on the campus. This is especially the case when the commitment of such a ministry allows an open appreciation of secular resources and secular formulations of human problems. One has to remember the difficulties that the university had in breaking loose from the dogmatic controls of religion. Assuming that the religious communities want not to control but to contribute, the university can be assisted by their participation in the campus scene.

Finally, there is a sense in which the formal ministry of religious institutions on the campus facilitates a ministry on the part of the university to the society as a whole. The religious ministry can provide a channel of communication that allows the university to be understood for what it is and helps the society assimilate and adjust creatively to technological change. Such a channel should be a means of interpreting the importance of such concepts as academic freedom. It should feed the novel and crucial developments from the university into the very structure of our religious bodies so they will be better prepared to deal intelligently and openly with the unique and challenging developments of our future. It is not only the President of the United States who needs some kind of consensus. The university needs it too, not so it can survive or keep its status, but so that its contributions, its ideas, its knowledge can be put to work in the life and direction of our society.

This channel of communication is important not only for the positive transmissions that may take place. It is also of vital importance for broad sections of our society to understand the problems that the university is up against. An example of this may be seen in the Berkeley revolt, where the fact that the university had its problems was made clear. When the Berkeley students protested, it was of real value to our churches that some ministers and campus workers were closely enough involved to give a constructive and fair interpretation of these events to the churches and their leadership. As in so many situations, the reports one reads in the newspapers and the attitudes expressed by a frightened society are not adequate for a total understanding of the issues involved. One can imagine other situations in which it would be a real advantage, for both the university and the church, to have a person representing the church on the scene.

In these ways the formal ministry has an important role to play on the campus. None of these functions give that ministry a controlling voice. They do allow for persuasive contact with individuals, groups, and the institution itself. In that contact, the door is at least open to the possibility that religious commitment is ultimately a creative and liberating dynamic that is of vital relevance to students and society.

And this is the point where the student came in.

The Silent Sixties?*

JOHN H. CUSHMAN AND LAWRENCE SUSSKIND

* This article is an attempt to formulate some conclusions and present some insights into our generation. It is about university students, written by university students, and includes references to those authors whose comments seem to us to be pertinent.

Our society is being transformed at a startling rate; economic growth and cybernation have transfigured our environment, and nowhere more than in the urban university are the effects and implications of this change so obvious. We have read the macabre prediction that in the future "every student will have a keyboard connected to a central computer; he will then be able to have a give-and-take discourse with this electronic scholar." But if such an event is the end of communication, then certainly it is just that.

Nowhere else are the fears, anxieties, hopes, and ideologies of the future more apparent than in the lives of the college students in the urban universities today. The university is the prototype of the future city, and if we are concerned with shaping the growth of the society, it must be to the university that we turn for example; it is to the student we turn for study.

What kind of person is the university student of the 1960s? He is a young person who has proved his intellectual capabilities and his individual talents even before entering college. He has a great, even excessive, awareness of the complexities that surround him; he is well read and well informed, and he is decent in his personal relations. The college youth is deeply committed, passionately involved—and this underscores his desperate drive for communication. Whether a student is committed to CORE, HEP, a citizenship program, SNCC, Students for a Democratic Society, his fraternity, his football team, or his studies, or any combination of these, he is passionately involved. Such involvement forms the values upon which he will bet the rest of his life.

Is the student of the sixties alienated, as so many sociologists have implied? Alienation implies alienation *from* something; and the college student of the sixties is just not willing to accept the existence of a set of social values that apply to him. He is not alienated from a series of accepted norms, he is creating new norms for his own generation.

College students are optimistic, and many of us have forgotten how to cry for help. Frustration becomes action, not a whimpery passivity. We have been called a "great leisure class," though students admittedly lead a double or triple life. Supposedly we have a much easier situation than the nine-to-five job-holder. Unfortunately, we are not just job-holders any more, but persons genuinely interested in what we are doing. For us there is no incentive to join the economic rat race. We would like to think that what we are doing is meaningful, and perhaps we are still interested in the human race.

Are the conflicts new? Not entirely. They are new because they confront us individually for the first time, and they can be treated freshly because we have the experience of preceding generations. They are old because each generation has had its struggle for recognition apart from the established generation. But we are unsympathetic with elders who speak of science as just so much "sociologese-psychologese gobbledygook." Supposedly there is value in the pursuit of knowledge. We are interested in new words to increase the possibilities of communication; these new words are merely touchstones for new possibilities of thought. We are optimistic about the new possibilities.

A new ethic marked by both its irreverence and concern has evolved to replace the traditional Protestant ethic (a hard day's work for a hard day's pay). It questions such traditional hallmarks as Christianity, my country right or wrong, the sanctity of marriage and premarital chastity, civil disobedience, the accumulation of wealth, the right or even the competence of parents, the schools, and the government heads to make decisions for everyone.

Communication has always been a major concern for everyone, but communication today for the college student means something different from communication for the past generation. Postwar society was an alienated society. It was alienated from itself, and its people were alienated from one another; these were the "hollow men." The postwar student, with a terrifying past immediately behind him, needed to create an intellectual distance between himself and the objects he wanted to comprehend. This distance gave him a feeling of security. When one creates an artificial meaning to ease comprehension, it makes both people and events more real than they actually are, and though it eases comprehension, it creates a distance that increases noncommunication. The student of the sixties is trying desperately for a different kind of communication. He is a different kind of person and therefore requires a different mode of communication.

This new mode of communication is completely personalized. It is, in the words of Martin Buber, an I–Thou relationship, with no artificial distance hindering the dialogue. There is a vast verbal underground among university students, riddled with phrases and intonations that communicate the most basic emotions, likes, and dislikes. There must be a reason why highly educated young people are resorting to a continually changing glossary. When students, wrapped up in the highly intellectualized and idealized language of their studies, continually modify their speech, it is because they desire to communicate with the people around them. In a highly technical and changing environment, language changes too. Students are especially sensitive to this modulation; they are also aware of the meaninglessness that characterizes the language of their elders. Students are trying to speak with one another, actually communicate. Although slavery has always existed, it has never been so differentiated, encompassed so many vocabularies, or changed with such rapidity.

The generation prior to ours was moderate and privatistic; it has been called the "silent fifties." The affinity for the problems of one's peers in the university today may be called a consciousness of consciousness, an awareness not only of the other person as he affects me, but an awareness of his own consciousness of himself. This consciousness goes a long way toward explaining the whys of thought and action of today's university student.

The world is no longer sacred. Instead of a mysterious world incomprehensible to society, we live in a world that is scientifically explainable: religious mysteries have been replaced by secular problems. It is possible that there is another reformation currently taking place in organized religion, but it would be difficult to trace its beginnings to a single event such as the posting of the Ninety-five Theses by Martin Luther in 1517. When a religious book other than the Bible becomes a best-seller there is reason to believe that the book might tell us more about "the market than the product."

John Robinson, author of *Honest to God*, is honest in his approach to theology. Let's face it, baby, God just isn't talking to people face to face any more. It's getting tougher and tougher to have an honest-to-goodness revelation. His theology challenges traditional church dogma and its relevance to the modern world.

Inquiries into the nature of God, the universe, and their relationship to man have taken on new meaning in the last two decades. The Russians sent a man into space less than ten years ago. He radioed back to earth that he had circled the earth once every hour and a half for days, but nowhere in space could he find God. The church that has always hindered the advancement of science is now being turned upon by her retarded child. While there is value in studying religions for their historical content, the important problems of being seem to depend upon the way in which we use the science and theology of today to understand, in Paul Tillich's words, "the God beyond God." The physical accomplishments of our times make little difference if man loses his soul to the computer, and thus contemporary problems demand a contemporary religion.

Recently we attended a worship service conducted entirely in the folk idiom. The traditional "Onward Christian Soldiers" was replaced by a hymn sung to the tune of "This Land Is Your Land," accompanied by guitar, bass, and banjo. The leader sang the call to worship accompanied by a twelve-string guitar, and the confessional litany was a responsive hymn, again accompanied by guitar. The prayers were taken from newspaper headlines: PRESIDENT JOHNSON HAS AFFIRMED THIS COUNTRY'S WILLINGNESS TO DECLARE A TEMPORARY TRUCE IN VIETNAM OVER THE CHRISTMAS AND

NEW YEAR'S HOLIDAY and WOMAN JUMPS FROM EIGHTH STORY OF BUILDING HOLDING CHILD. We pray for these people and other people like them, and like ourselves. Seven Negro children read and acted out the Biblical story of the Prodigal Son: the New Testament reading. The story seemed relevant. The sermon was a dramatic reading. Three men assumed the roles of people who had actually participated in the events described, and positioned themselves in three areas in front of, behind, and on the side of the seated congregation. All felt involved in the allegorical story being sermonized. For the final hymn we sang "He's got the whole world in his hands" and were asked to shake hands with everybody we could reach. We did.

This service was an attempt at communication among people who have grown up with folk songs, with front pages of the newspaper, and shaking the hands of new friends. The service was the most successful we have ever attended in terms of involving the congregation in a communication among themselves. If such communication constitutes a religious experience, it was achieved. Older people smiled at us as we sang the 100th Psalm with guitar accompaniment; some were offended at this violation of the sacred traditional service. But the college students, who made up the majority of the congregation, left with a religious experience tucked somewhere down inside them.

Martin Buber accurately describes the meaningful relationships that exist among people, the world, and the interaction of the two. Most relationships are those which take place between a person and a thing. Under such conditions a person uses the thing as a tool, and as a means for furthering his own personal gain. Such a relationship is between I and It. Usually these "things" include the people with whom we have a common working experience. The I–It relationship is too often the teacher-student relationship, and the relationship with a world that seems to be controlled for human purposes. But the real communicative relationship is between I and Thou. *Thou* is a sacred term reserved only for those who are meaningful in and of themselves; who are not used, but who share with you. Before proceeding further, it is important to see that this may be the purpose of communication: to achieve an understanding based not upon the value of a person as a tool, but as a human being with whom one may share experiences. This may be expanded to include not only an understanding of the person as he affects me, but an understanding of the motivations of his actions: a consciousness of his own consciousness. The I–Thou may be only a fleeting experience, possibly only a moment of total understanding, but nevertheless a goal worth pursuing.

Direct connection between the I–Thou experience and the consciousness-expanding (psychedelic) drugs may be seen. "Suddenly I saw my own hands in a strange new way, and when I touched her I felt that I was not touching merely skin, but a human being; I was conscious of her being," said an LSD experimenter. LSD experimenters claim amazing perception of the true nature of that with which they come into contact. Some psychedelic experiences producing an I–Thou relationship with the world may be viewed as religious. It is curious that William James' popular title of the early 1900s, *Varieties of Religious Experience*, has been replaced by *Varieties of Psychedelic Experience* in the sixties. Far from being a play on words, this title comments upon the very essence of the religious experience: consciousness of the self in relation to the universe.

As students we tend not to accept the traditional definitions but rather try to search out definitions in context. A definition out of context is meaningless. Many ask what the function of religion is today, and what the purpose of religious behavior is. Sure I believe in God, who is he? Or rather what is it? We are faced not only with the problems of applying the functions and purposes of religion to the dilemmas of the model community, but also with the task of connecting God with these religious ideas.

After depositing the white-bearded God of our childhood on the steps of the library, we went inside and began looking up definitions: the Protestant definition, the Jewish definition, the Catholic definition, the Buddhist definition, the definition of the death of God. In frustration, we wanted to return to the steps of the library to search for our white-bearded God.

Perhaps the college student would like to go back to the traditional religious forms that offer him security, but modern science and the modern university are not willing to grant a student the comfortable posture of living among the definitions of the past. If students find honesty in the struggle with the "ultimate concerns," it will be impossible to agree that God is dead. We are searching for a "God beyond God," and a God that will give meaning to the relationships of this world.

Students seek concrete experiences that in quantity will form a common ground for communication. Experimentation with drugs in the form of "tripping" is communicative. Widespread interest in the exact nature of tripping has developed with the rise in the use of psychedelic drugs such as LSD, mescalin, psilocybin, hashish, and marijuana. Two things must be made very clear: first, it is impossible to pin down the exact number and percentage of students who are experimenting with these drugs. The report of the New York Medical Society's subcommittee on narcotics addiction is skeptical about the 20-to-50-per cent estimate of students in college having experience with marijuana. But whatever the exact figure, we can safely guarantee that the figure is rising. There are more users now than there were a year ago, or two years ago, or fifteen years ago. It is impossible to determine the number of users or experimenters, for many students will confess an experience with marijuana even though they have never really had one. This is an important point to recognize: talk of experimentation serves as a means of dialogue for students.

The second point is that "tripping" is nothing more than a metaphor used to describe a personal experience. Tripping is the means of freedom from the constraints and internalized anxieties that have characterized so many personal relationships of the past. Dr. Timothy Leary (whatever else he may claim to be) is one of the leading authorities on tripping. He points out the negative attitudes that occur during and after a trip: the loss of rationality, fear of acting shamelessly, terror of really seeing yourself, disenchantment with society, discovery of an abnormal world that seems more attractive than the rational world; all of these are possibilities. Yet there are also positive results that the user hopes to attain: transcendence of hidden fears; truthful, intuitive behavior; hope of really finding one's self; insight into the inner workings of the society; the hope of seeing more creative alternatives; the attainment of a realm of awareness which will transform everything into a world of delight.

The majority of usage is limited to experimentation. Even in a situation such as that of Columbia University, located in the midst of a city in which drugs, although illegal, are readily accessible, there are few hard-core users—mainly because they could not survive in the academic world if they were. Since neither marijuana ("pot") nor LSD ("acid") is habit-forming, there is no danger of being hooked, as there is with heroin.

To be sure, there are dangers inherent in the use of marijuana and LSD. There is the possibility of intensifying emotional imbalance already present in an immature, unstable personality. However, the real significance of the increase in experimentation with drugs is the attempt on the part of the students to keep from being estranged from persons and values important to them. They are taking a risk in attempting to discover permanent and meaningful relationships, experimenting in order to create a common ground of experience.

Equality and tolerance are necessary parts of this new consciousness, and there is an honest disposition to it that permits things and relationships to just happen without deliberate forethought and planning. This new honesty can be seen in writing, theatre, music, and painting.

Pop art, such as the work of Andy Warhol, shows us that the ordinary things we sometimes disregard (junk items, old newspapers, Coke bottles, tin cans) can be assembled artistically. The whole of life is subject matter for a communal creativity. All too often we dismiss this art as being too personal and therefore too obscure to lend itself to interpretation. Pop and op art are often considered incomprehensible, and when an apparent representation is not within our easy reach, a shrug of the shoulders (usually accompanied with a remark along the lines of "that artist doesn't really communicate an idea; it's too personal, or it's a hoax") is the result.

Pop art is not a hoax. In fact, the pop and op artists have been bold enough to do what we have not been able to find the courage to do. These artists are the first to be skeptical of the modern science; they do not assume that change is necessarily good, and that artificial plastic forms must be the ultimate creation of the human race. Pop and op art should be taken seriously, but understood for what they are: tongue-in-cheek reflections of the absurdity of our scientific race to noncreativity. The new art forms are a kind of uninhibited play; they don't pretend to apply order or form to a chaotic existence. They are mocking that existence that most of us readily accept as virtuous.

With the development of pop and op art and the institution of psychedelic art, an attempt at an even deeper communication is obvious. We have moved full circle from abstraction: pop and op art rely on the most basic forms of all, the most real. A Campbell's soup can, a burned mattress, or geometric formulas are not in the least abstract; they are elements we have always had to cope with. As art forms they carry with them the most authentic communication the artist has yet been able to render.

The art form of the present and the future is the "happening" —the creation of environmental art. A happening is an assemblage of events performed in more than one time and place. The inventor of the happening, or perhaps its discoverer, Allen Kaprow, says, "A happening's material environment may be constructed, taken over directly from what is available, or altered slightly; just as its activities may be invented or commonplace. A happening, unlike a stage play, may occur at a supermarket, driving along a highway, under a pile of rags, and in a friend's kitchen. The happening is performed according to plan but without rehearsal, audience, or repetition. It is art, but seems closer to life." Besides happening, in the Kaprow form, modern theatre has tended to move in this direction. The dramatists we have so unkindly labeled "absurd," such as Ionesco, Genêt, Pinter, Adamov, and Beckett, are not nonsense authors. Rather, they write about the nonsense of human existence; they do not extol the patterned virtues of their society but reveal the dilemmas of humanity. They communicate not only with sight and sound, but with a conscious attempt at honest psychological representation.

The poetry of Allen Ginsberg is a modern example of dedication of consciousness. The "cut-up" technique that he employs amasses the reactions of all the senses simultaneously. What is seen, what is felt, what he can smell, taste, and remember are pieced together in a random order:

I wandered in and out of the brilliant stacks of cans following in you, and followed in my imagination by the store detective. We strode down the open corridors together in our solitary fancy tasting artichokes, possessing every frozen delicacy, and never passing the cashier.

Where are we going, Walt Whitman? The doors close in an hour. Which way does your beard point tonight?

(I touch your book and dream of your odyssey in the supermarket and feel absurd.)

Will we walk all night through solitary streets? The trees add shade to shade, lights out in the houses, we'll both be lonely.*

As the poet describes that feeling of oneness, he administers to the truth, and lays his soul on the line in an open attempt at communication. Poetry is the power to create, and in conferring a new meaning on a subject, the contemporary poet—and similarly the contemporary composer, painter, and writer—is begging for an active and complete dialogue. In the presentation of what is real he is seeking a bridge: a meaningful construction that will escape from a previous alienation, dishonesty, and loneliness.

Students are concerned with the indifference and lack of faith that characterize so many of the relationships within the society

* From "A Supermarket in California."

at large. This concern leads them to question and challenge the traditional values and standards handed down to them by their parents and Dr. Spock. More than anything else, parent-child relationships exhibit faithlessness and loveless dialogue. Parents barter with their children: you do this for me, and I'll do this for you. "If you want me to take you to your friend's house, you had better do this for me right now." Even worse than the business aspect is the fact that parents expect their children to provide a "profit on their investment." They expect their children to do better than they did.

Students have been forsaken; they have been taught right and wrong as much as they have been taught "profitable" and "unprofitable." They have been forced to work out their own ways of dealing with their personal and sexual relationships. This has led many to a situational approach that means, in some situations, anything goes—you meet the demands of the other person —in other cases you do not. There is, however, one norm that has remained unchanged. This, I think, is a fact that has been termed the New Morality, a norm that has been absent in many parent-child relationships. The norm that remains intact is *love*. Most students will agree: it is foolish to suggest that love for another person can only be present when the sex act takes place between persons who are legally married. Students have begun to regulate themselves according to their own intuition and impulses; they are more realistic, responsible, and serious than they are given credit for. In the world of the university, promiscuity is not applauded. Promiscuity is not the essential character of the New Morality, as so many adults have inferred. Promiscuity is still present, but no more so than in earlier times.

Students don't just think they are adults, they *are* adults. Our parents pushed us out of adolescence when we left home for college. Perhaps this is the result of abundance, perhaps a result of the rapid pace of life in a technical environment; it might be attributed to the thought that you are required to give your life to your country at age eighteen. Contemporary lovers may move from first encounter to complete intimacy with an alacrity that astounds their elders, but this is not to be judged as widespread promiscuity. People function naturally in relationship to other people, and functioning apart from other people does not occur now. Since the student is separated from his family in the university, he needs to relate to the people in his new environment. In terms of this type of involvement love still stands as the stabilizing norm. Love represents a total understanding, a profound involvement and concern, and this seems to characterize the communication young people are striving for today.

No longer are college students joining groups in the hope of finding an identity in which to shroud themselves, nor are they doing something because it is the "in" thing to do. They leave that to their parents. Group orientation is a natural orientation. However, the expressions *gang behavior* or *group identity* do not work as satisfactory explanations of present patterns of behavior. College students enter into group relationships and one-to-one relationships because within them they expect to find a common environment of expression. People with the same attitudes supporting similar causes would, it seems likely, have a greater opportunity for complete dialogue. Therefore *group identity*, if we must continue to use the term, represents not an answer or supplement to a student who has no personality, but, on the contrary, a meeting ground for students who bring established attitudes and ideals with them into fluid environments that favor communication.

Interpersonal relationships are characterized, then, by their frankness and concern. It is true that very often sexual relationships are characterized by an absolute lack of faith and a purely physical domination. In these cases one is perfectly aware of what he is doing, and recognizes his conquest only as a means of dialogue with his partner. But this is not the essential character of the personalized relationships that don't pretend to be anything else. These have always existed. Those people we choose to love and care about are the people with whom we develop the relationships characterized by the new mode of personal involvement, and this involvement need no longer be sanctified by marriage.

Student involvement entails a great deal. The declaration of the Students for a Democratic Society (Port Huron) seeks the establishment of a democracy characterized by individual participation and governed by two central aims: "that the individual share in those social decisions determining the quality and direction of his life; that society be organized to encourage independence in men and to provide the media for their common participation." This generation focuses on civil rights, peace, and poverty, but beyond these there is a force working to give a greater meaning and participation to all people.

Rarely in the United States have young people had a share in the formulation of their future, and only occasionally have they even felt that they had a right to ask for a part in these decisions. At Berkeley in California and at Columbia in New York, students seek a voice in university decisions: faculty tenure, tuition raises, military recruitment and training on campus, and acceptance of Defense Department research grants. The faculty have supported student demands in both schools. It is hard to learn about the benefits of representation and then spend four years without those benefits.

We do not wish to imply that anyone with interest is necessarily part of the active student movement. The candor implicit in the modern movement is not always obvious. Many students who are concerned are not actively involved. What does involvement entail? In order to keep up with the transformation of our society, a unique personality is required. To deal with the shifting events and trends a greater flexibility is required; and, the rate of exchange being what it is, the highly educated must be able to shift with the changing technology.

The active student groups are not bands of rabblerousers wandering from cause to cause looking for something to yell about. Student involvement is not an outlet for the tension built up by studies, the bomb, or anything else. An examination of various groups and individuals on the New Left reveals a definite adherence to structure, definite goals, and planning for the future; an orientation that demands faith and serious consideration.

What, in the student's terms, is a successful political involvement? More important, what constitutes success? Ostensibly, it appears that success continues to be measured not in our own terms, but more in our parents' terms. The student struggles; the student whose parents still manipulate the strings holds grades in high esteem because these grades guarantee pride, satisfaction, and acceptance when he returns home. But alone on the campus, he needs to be in communication with his fellows; grades are a poor substitute for meaningful relationships. The college student is not so willing to pretend that an academic degree and a place in the rat race constitute success; he is not willing to stake all his security on possessions. He is unwilling to delude himself, and because of this competition in the university has become meaningful.

His disillusionment with the system results primarily from the hypocrisy that he has been forced to deal with for so long. After so many years of hearing on the one hand how important it is to be "true to yourself, honest, well-rounded, and working to your limits" and on the other that "it's a dog-eat-dog existence and only the strongest, fittest, succeeds," one tends to throw up his hands, sit down on the curb, and wonder if there isn't some solution.

Outside, in the competitive capitalistic society, everyone is constantly threatened by circumstances or by other people. In the university a community exists; each individual competes in some sense, but each is very aware of the fact that without communal cooperation the university will be defeating itself. Everyone has to work together, it is almost impossible to work against anyone in the university and succeed. This to some extent explains the commitment of the college student and many of the reasons why university students have found satisfaction in political affiliations. Involvement is the solution to many of the problems that have plagued the past.

Today man is free: free to compete in the capitalistic society, free to be estranged, alienated, miserable; free to feel insecure, impotent, and lonely. Political-group orientation allows for complete communication and the satisfaction of group expression and the security and understanding that go with it. When there is fear among people they mistrust one another, and consequently do not speak to one another. Political groups have created a unified voice, an aggregate of distinct personal opinions that speaks with no hint of temerity, and with obvious trust and honesty.

We have been talking about change and communication. I think that if I hear one more after-dinner speaker say "The problems of this generation are not different from the problems of my generation; I have faith that these kids are no different than we were . . ." I will probably have to leave the table. We come to college to prepare ourselves for the values and relationships of the adult world. If these are changing values based upon increasing knowledge, then they must be different from those of the generation that preceded us. No doubt they will be different in the generation to follow. But now we must be selfishly concerned with the communication among our own generation. Student interest in politics, newspaper headlines, and radical theology seems radical only to those who will not accept change. Students feel that the changes and decisions they are making are of value, or they would not experiment with them; it is not our purpose to argue for the sake of argument, but to argue for the sake of improvement.

We feel that the greatest improvements have come in the expansion of communication. We have considered attempts to achieve greater responsiveness in art, in poetry, and in religion. Many will feel uneasy when they see the beloved traditions of the past altered, but they are altered only in attempt to achieve a purer form. Hopefully, the pure forms are unattainable, and will cause us to continue to search for new and better means of communication to reach them. Contemplation of the pure forms is the greatest good of which man is capable; Plato said that. Change does not breed security, and, most assuredly, it does not breed silence.

Epilogue

CHAPLAIN JOHN D. CANNON

CAMPUS clergy frequently find themselves invited by agencies outside academia—civic associations, men's and women's clubs, church and synagogue groups—to interpret the turbulent university scene, and, in particular, to describe campus religious life. We have learned to expect that there will always be present in a particular group a handful of ancient alumni and anxious parents who refuse to accept the fact that anything has changed. They prefer to believe that celebrated instances of campus upheaval are "typical" and "timeless" and certainly avoidable if the chaplains had been doing their job.

Unfortunately public attention has been pruriently focused on a so-called "morals revolution," which according to some sources of information originates on the campus. Many parents seem to be fascinated by the thought that campus extracurricular life revolves around the "orgy" and the "trip"—sexual extravagances and drug-induced excursions into inner cellular space. Coupled with the assumption that the campus is controlled by bearded beatniks intent on generating discontent, these impressions create a smoke screen of prurient fantasies, vicious lies, and diabolical half-truths, through which it is difficult—if not impossible—to discern the dynamic and exciting realities of contemporary campus life.

The purpose of the authors has been to pierce this smoke screen from within and to expose to the public something of the vitality of the university scene, particularly as it affects the shape and style of campus ministry. The traditional image of the university campus as a sort of serene Eden wherein the fruits of learning are ritually enjoyed in a time-tested transition from the innocence of youth to the sophistication of the adult world has been shattered. Gone as well is the complementary image of the college chaplain as a guardian of traditional virtues, a godly guide who accompanies the young through the trials of adolescence and intellectual growth. Instead we are confronted with the multiversity—a highly secularized educational city that Clark Kerr has described as "a series of processes producing a series of results—held together by administrative rules and powered by money." It is no wonder then that campus ministers are no longer able to function according to the expectations of those whose vision of higher education is defined by Fraternity Row and compulsory chapel.

In this regard, it is startling for those of us whose ministry is at Columbia University to recall the intentions of the venerable ecclesiastical benefactors who founded this institution slightly more than two hundred years ago. In an advertisement in the *New York Mercury* on June 3, 1754, the formation of the College of New York was announced as follows:

The chief thing that is aimed at in this College, is, to teach and engage the Children to know God in Jesus Christ, and to love and serve him in all Sobriety, Godliness, and Righteousness of Life, with a perfect Heart and a willing mind; and to train them up in all virtuous Habits, and all such useful Knowledge, as may render them creditable to their Families and Friends, Ornaments to their country, and useful to the publick Weal in their generations.

Little did this devout cleric suspect that this child of Christian culture would cast off its religious swaddling clothes and emerge as a soulless giant. Clearly it was supposed that the established order of society—an order wherein Church, Crown, and College were divinely ordained to represent among men the Priestly, Kingly, and Prophetic functions of Christ—would endure until Kingdom Come. The campus without religion was inconceivable. Indeed the campus was conceived as a training ground for the Christian scholar and gentleman.

We would be less than honest were we not to admit that there are many in the secular university for whom the chaplain is the superfluous keeper of a relic—the curator of an ancient tradition and the advocate of interests which are as archaic as the *Mercury* advertisement. He must be confined to the chapel, they say, except for public ceremonies when he is permitted to pay homage to the harmless corpse of Christian culture. Let us admit also that we continue to hear sad sounds from Mother Church—the wail of those who shudder to think that Alma Mater has been raped by Modernity and who complain to the campus minister that he should launch a new crusade to reclaim the university for the church. But these are the lesser voices.

What we mainly hear is the eloquent silence of those who are sufficiently sophisticated to know that we are no longer—especially not in the contemporary university—surrounded by a Christian or a religious culture. They are usually too kind to be contemptuous of clergy and too clever to request their services —unless they want to get married or buried. Religious ministers are marginal. The ministries sought after by secular man—and most of our students and faculty do not define themselves in any other terms—are the passionate presence of peers, the professional methods of therapists and personnel workers, and—above all, in the university, the disciplined dispenser of knowledge and technique.

One would suppose then that campus clergy would beat a quick retreat to more fertile fields where shepherds of the spirit continue as pillars of the community. Indeed, St. Stalemate in Suburbia seems sometimes like a distant Paradise. If religious culture is "no longer" there, then at least secular culture is "not yet," and the calm between the storms is inviting. But we have the comfort on campus of knowing that if we can't make it here, where the shape of the future is already emerging, then we might as well abandon the ship of faith before it is too late. It is increasingly evident to us that if religious institutions have a future in Western society, then they must demonstrate viability within the secular university. We must learn to prove the faith to a new generation. We must firm up and flesh out the dry bones of our tradition by imbibing deeply of the spirit and thought of our age, and that is the opportunity that excites us daily as campus ministers.

We have license and not infrequently a mandate from religious agencies to play down specifically denominational and parochial interests and to discover roles for ourselves within the context of higher education which are constructive, creative, and consistent with our faith-commitment. We are no longer inclined to assume the posture of Mother's Man on Campus. Nor are we willing to give priority to ecclesiastical mandates which call for the establishment of religious "clubs," catering to the needs of the faithful and fearful who would retreat from a world come of age into a home-away-from-home. Neither are we prepared to serve strictly as the smiling superintendent of a campus religious enclave, blissfully unaware of the world we live in. As the authors have indicated, like any other mature adult in an academic community we are still asked to act as a parent-surrogate in times of stress and strain. And we continue to exercise conventional sacramental ministries, like parish clergy. But we do not pretend that these services exhaust the possibilities for ministry in higher education.

Given the absence of a precise mandate from either church or university or of any compelling model, it is clear that no two campus clergy are going to have the same priorities or style. At Columbia where Roman Catholic, Jewish, and Protestant clergy work together as an interfaith ministry, each of the religious counselors (as they are called) tends to focus on a particular sector of university life, according to his special talents and inclinations. Thus there are several points of view represented in these pages, reflecting the orientation of the particular author. Clearly a "coffee-house" ministry is specialized and has obvious limitations. As much as anything it has become a symbol of the fact that our interests extend beyond the sanctuary and that we want to be present with students where they are and share their concerns, their pleasures, and their trials. Similarly, the student radical and the new activist engage our interest. If several of the counselors make common cause with these students it is because their interests often converge as they confront the pressing social problems of our time and seek to discover ways of participating responsibly and effectively in the society they have inherited. Then, also, there continue to be students with more traditional interests. They ask not only the familiar questions of the college student—Who am I? What will I do? Where do I belong? How do I decide?—but they ask these agonizing questions against the background of religious training and in the face of searching intellectual challenges to faith and belief. Very often this religious training has been authoritatively imposed with little attempt to win the mind as well as the heart. More often than not it was thoroughly inadequate to survive a liberal education. Thus we recognize a special responsibility in the contemporary university to provide a context in which faith and learning can meet and grow together.

Several assumptions shared by all the clergy at Columbia bind us together despite our differences of style and perspective. *We accept the fact that the particular cultural epoch, at least as it embraces us in the secular university, is post-religious.* We recognize the fact that the consciousness of the Western intellectual—and increasingly of Western man in general—is not determined by a compelling and coherent system of religious doctrines, moral demands, sacred observances—by creeds, codes, and cult.

Whereas the college used to be the context in which one became indoctrinated into and trained for leadership in the religious culture, it now functions as a context in which a transition from the residual religious culture to a secular culture is accomplished. The student is still trained for leadership but his character model is no longer the eighteenth-century scholar-gentleman. Excellence is defined instead in terms of intellectual proficiency and technical ability. What is valued is the ability to "make it" and this applies to social future as well as individual destiny. Knowledge is the means and the only accepted end is living itself. Thus the classroom and the extra-curriculum serve as a series of trials in which the student develops ego strength and mental acumen. If he has effective needs that the peer group cannot satisfy or that cannot be sublimated in athletic or artistic activities, he has available professional therapists who can assist him with his unfinished childhood business.

This, of course, is secularity with a vengeance. And when we say that we accept it, we do not mean that we condone it. Neither do we condemn it. We have no vested interest—even as clergymen—in "things as they used to be." Nor are we inclined to resign ourselves to things as they are, just because they're happening. If we live in a postreligious age, it is still as men of faith. And if faith means anything in this context, it suggests that a commitment has been made, against which all other claims on the person are evaluated. Our participation in faith communities provides us with an historical perspective that is not determined by the insight of the moment, but by the cumulative experience of a people, wrestling through successive cultural epochs with the problems of human existence. Thus the criteria that determine our evaluation of the present stage of culture transcend the particular situation in which we find ourselves. We are bound to be critical, therefore, even as we participate in our own times and appreciate life as it is lived today. As campus ministers we regard it as our function to demonstrate by the sincerity and depth of our participation in the university, that faith is not false or fatal for contemporary man. It is our task to show that faith can be articulated intelligibly—that it can be reasonable. We attempt to demonstrate that the life of faith is a live option even for postreligious man, indeed that it can provide the individual with a perspective that is both appreciative of the past, creatively critical of the present, and confident of man's capacity to shape and enjoy his future.

This is not to suggest that we are intent on imposing our own commitments on the unwilling or willing. We are not interested in advancing a particular faith to the exclusion of all others. *We accept the emergence of radical pluralism as a welcome change from the domination of culture by a single ideology or religion.* We take it to be one of our tasks to provide resources whereby the student can learn not only tolerance but appreciation of cultural and religious diversity. Hence our programs are increasingly oriented to interreligious study and discussion, and to dialogue with secular communities and disciplines. What we wish to demonstrate is that particular and passionate loyalties can exist amicably together and benefit from conversational exchange, mutual ethical and cultural activities, and theological cross-fertilization.

Finally, *we share the assumption that our ministry is within and to the total university.* As I have indicated we do not regard ourselves as agents of interests that are inimicable to higher education. Nor are we interested in catering to a pious minority within the undergraduate ranks of the institution. Although we spend most of our time with students, we do not exclude from our realm of interest faculty, administrative personnel and employees. Our interest is not in persons to the exclusion of policies —whether these involve the relationship of higher education to society, the content of course offerings, the design of housing accommodations, or the ethics of contracted research. This is troubling to those who prefer that the clergyman confine himself to his particular realm of expertise—namely the language and practice of the cult, and the cure of souls. We recognize that we are no longer regarded as spiritual and moral exemplars, except to those who share our commitments. Indeed it would be presumptuous for us to claim to be the conscience or "soul" of the institution. The secular university is not lacking in ethically sensitive and morally concerned individuals who struggle daily with the consequences for human life of educational processes and institutional policies. Nevertheless we assume that we have a special responsibility for raising questions of value and meaning and for understanding and articulating the problems and pitfalls which attend and threaten individual and corporate life. So too we assume that it is incumbent on us to expose the prejudices and pathologies which influence attitudes and behavior. In this regard we are likely to appear as vigorous critics not only of social and educational institutions in general, but of the religious communities in which we hold membership.

At Columbia, the campus ministers are designated as "religious counselors." This suggests that they are expected to give priority to the problems of persons, insofar as these relate to the "religious" dimension of human existence. Certainly adjustment problems, issuing from the relationship of the individual to some aspect of his religious heritage, continue to command our attention. Such problems include the observance of dietary laws, conflicts between inherited taboos and peer-group sanctions, and the necessity of re-examining cherished values and beliefs in the light of new insights and knowledge.

But the religious counselor increasingly spends his time attending to concerns and questions which are not so explicitly related to code, creed, and cult. It is evident from these chapters that his interests encompass problems and inquiry of broader existential import. All behavior reflects commitments whether these are accidental or intentional, conscious or unwitting. So we find ourselves called upon to assist members of the academic community as they seek to clarify their values, to identify the criteria that govern decisions, and to organize and integrate insight and information into a coherent whole. Not infrequently problems emerge as an individual is sensitized to and confronts an issue or a particular situation requiring a response. These may range from relationships with the local draft board to relationships with parents and peers—from war to love. More often than not we do not have pat answers nor do we dispense them on demand even when we do have them. At best, we attempt to assist the individual in seeing his own problems and questions in a broader perspective, which includes the possible consequences of a choice or of inaction both to himself and to society.

As the authors have indicated, we have now begun to move in new directions. Our work, to be sure, is both exploratory and experimental. For over a hundred years religious institutions have been on the defensive in the face of cultural and intellectual upheavals and technological innovation. Today we find ourselves aligned with significant numbers of students and faculty within the university who are passionately intent on discovering what it means to be human in a world "come of age" and how it is that we can affirm something of value in a world wherein nothing is sacred. We are confident that the present generation of students are spiritually alive in spite of and quite likely because of their worldliness. Our task, as campus clergy, is to accompany them and their mentors in this process of discovery, and to share their sufferings and joys. Increasingly we find that they welcome us as comrades and as concerned adults who are anxious to co-operate in forging a future.

ABOUT THE AUTHORS

ALBERT H. FRIEDLANDER, Associate Counselor to Jewish Students at Columbia University from 1961 to 1966, is at present living in England, where he is Rabbi of Wembley Liberal Synagogue, Chaplain to liberal Jewish students at Cambridge University, and Lecturer in History at the Leo Baeck College, London. He holds a Ph.D. from Columbia University and recently translated and edited Leo Baeck's *This People Israel: The Meaning of Jewish Existence.*

WILLIAM F. STARR is Protestant Counselor and Adviser to Episcopal Students at Columbia. A native of Connecticut, he received his B.A. from Yale in 1955 and his S.T.M. in Philosophy of Religion from General Theological Seminary in 1965, writing his thesis on Kierkegaard. In addition to his participation in the Protestant program, Mr. Starr is a candidate for the Ph.D. degree at Columbia University.

HENRY W. MALCOLM, Associate Counselor to Protestant Students and, since 1962, Presbyterian University Pastor, has also taken clinical pastoral training at Grady Memorial Hospital in Atlanta and studied for a year at the American Foundation for Religion and Psychiatry in New York City. At Columbia he has continued to pursue his interest in the application of psychoanalytic theory to social and educational problems.

JAMES EDWARD REA, born in New York City, was ordained in 1942 and received his Doctorate of Sacred Theology from the Catholic University of America. He was Professor of Theology from St. Joseph's Seminary before coming to Columbia in 1956, where he is Counselor to Catholic Students. Msgr. Rea has contributed to many popular and scholarly journals and is the author of *The Common Priesthood of the Members of the Mystical Body.*

LYMAN T. LUNDEEN is the Lutheran University Pastor and former Counselor to Protestant Students at Columbia. After three years as an officer with the USNR in the Korean War, he entered the Lutheran School of Theology at Chicago and earned his B.D. in 1960. While serving as Pastor of Lebanon Lutheran Church in West New York, New Jersey, he pursued postgraduate studies at Union Theological Seminary. Having received his S.T.M., Pastor Lundeen is a candidate for a Doctorate of Theology, and is preparing a thesis on Whitehead.

JOHN H. CUSHMAN majored in pre-medical studies as a member of the class of 1967 at Columbia College. LAWRENCE SUSSKIND, class of 1968, is a major in Sociology. Mr. Cushman is a member of the editorial staff, and Mr. Susskind is Editor, of *Sundial*, the literary magazine of Columbia University.

JOHN D. CANNON received his A.B. from Harvard College in 1956 and his B.D. from Union Theological Seminary in 1959. He came to Columbia in 1963 and participated for two years in the ministry of the Protestant Office before resigning this position to become Acting Chaplain of the University. In 1966 Chaplain Cannon began a three-year appointment as Chaplain of the University. He is Chairman of the Committee on Religious Life, formed by the President and trustees to undertake a comprehensive review of religious programs, procedures, and policies at Columbia; he serves also on the President's Committee on Student Life.

PAUL GOODMAN is the well-known author, critic, and educator whose books include *Growing Up Absurd, Kafka's Prayer, The Community of Scholars, The Empire City, Making Do, Compulsory Mis-Education,* and *Three Plays.* His most recent works, both published in 1967, are *Five Years* and *Like a Conquered Province: The Moral Ambiguity of America.*